THE WORLD AT THEIR FEET

THE WORLD AT THEIR FEET

NORTHERN IRELAND IN SWEDEN

RONNIE HANNA

SPORTS
BOOKS

Published by SportsBooks Ltd

Copyright: Ronnie Hanna © 2008
First published September 2008

SportsBooks Limited
PO Box 422
Cheltenham
GL50 2YN
United Kingdom
Tel: 01242 256755
Fax: 01242 254694
e-mail   randall@sportsbooks.ltd.uk
Website   www.sportsbooks.ltd.uk

Cover designed by Alan Hunns, Hunnsgraphics

Photo of Northern Ireland captain Danny Blanchflower and
coach Peter Doherty

A CIP catalogue record for this book is available from
the British Library.

ISBN 9781899807 74 1

Printed by Creative Print and Design, Wales

FOREWORD

It is a great pleasure and honour to write the foreword for this book about Northern Ireland's legendary 1958 World Cup team.

I was too young to see them play, but I've heard all the stories and read about their magnificent efforts fifty years ago in Sweden.

The 1958 World Cup was when the great Pelé announced himself on the global scene with outstanding performances that helped Brazil win the tournament.

It was also the competition that announced to the world that our wee country was not to be messed with.

They were good enough to come out of a group containing West Germany, Argentina and Czechoslovakia and make the quarter-finals.

The boys from that era were the first from Northern Ireland to qualify for a major finals and to reach the last eight really was something else.

I believe that every single player who has ever worn a Northern Ireland shirt since has been inspired by the legacy of the 1958 heroes.

For example look at 1982 and 1986 when we qualified for the World Cup finals again. Billy Bingham, who had played in 1958, was the manager in the '80s and was a marvellous motivator.

The names of 1958 are like a who's who of iconic Northern Ireland footballers. The likes of Harry Gregg, Danny Blanchflower, Bertie Peacock, Wilbur Cush, Jimmy McIlroy, Billy Bingham, Peter McParland and Derek Dougan are all legends.

I've been fortunate to meet some of the surviving members of the squad at various functions and they all talk about their World Cup experiences with great pride and joy. Listening to their stories makes me even more determined to follow in their footsteps and qualify for the World Cup.

They truly are an inspiration to us all.

David Healy

CONTENTS

Acknowledgements

A number of people and organisations have offered invaluable assistance in the writing of this book, but none have been more important than the interviewees from the Northern Ireland team of 1958: Billy Bingham, Harry Gregg, Jimmy McIlroy, Peter McParland and Norman Uprichard. I would like to thank them for their kind hospitality and their generosity with their time.

Two other gentlemen from that era – followers of rather than members of the team – also shared their memories of the time, and also loaned me some precious international programmes. My thanks go to Desmond Mitchell and Jim Storey for their help.

One of the unforeseen bonuses of writing this book has been making contact with Jonny Dewart who is responsible for one of the best websites about Northern Ireland international football – 'NIFG: Northern Ireland's Footballing Greats'. Jonny has provided a number of the illustrations featured here, going to a lot of time and trouble to do so. It has been a real privilege to have his support and interest.

Malcolm Brodie, that doyen of Northern Ireland football writers, Scotsman though he is, provided important information and contacts, and I have made liberal use of his contributions to the *Belfast Telegraph* in the 1950s.

Michael Boyd, IFA Head of Community Relations, has been unfailingly supportive, always expeditious – and courteous with it. I hope the Irish Football Association realise what a valuable asset they have in Michael.

My thanks, too, go to his IFA colleague Geoff Wilson, Head of Marketing and Communications, for providing some useful contacts. One of those contacts was Robert Park, to whom I am grateful for assisting with some of the final pieces to be put in place in the book.

I must pay due acknowledgement to the contribution of my publisher, Randall Northam. His experience and input has been a resource to which I have been very fortunate to have had access.

My wife Lorraine has also played her part, typing the lion's share of the original manuscript and reading the final draft for typos and faulty grammar. I left her plenty of scope to demonstrate her talent as a proofreader and my debt to her is a very real one.

In terms of organisations, I would like to thank the staff of the Irish and Local Studies Library in Armagh and Belfast Central Library's Newspaper Library. These were the locations for much of the core research for this book, and the prompt and efficient service that I experienced made the task all the more enjoyable.

Finally, my thanks to David Healy for providing the foreword for this book. I can pay him no higher compliment than to say that he was the missing element in that 1958 side – a goalscorer of international quality. In any event, if he has enjoyed reading this book half as much as I have enjoyed writing it, then he needs no further commendation.

Ronnie Hanna
Portadown
April 2008

PREFACE

CONFLICT AND ART

To travel back to the early 1950s, when this story begins, is to step as it were into a different world.

In October 1951, when Northern Ireland played their first game under Peter Doherty as manager, two of the wartime 'Big Three' were still forces to be reckoned with: Churchill was to return as prime minister at the end of the month, while Stalin remained all-powerful in the USSR. In the United States, Harry Truman was president, and Richard Nixon and John F. Kennedy had just entered the US Senate. Britain still had an empire, though the fault lines were beginning to appear (what we now know as the Commonwealth Games were in 1958 the Empire Games); continental Europe and now the Far East, where fighting continued in Korea, was frozen in the Cold War. Communist China, under Mao Tse Tung, was still in its infancy but was now a participant in the Korean War.

It was the year that saw the publication of Nicholas Monsarrat's classic story of the Atlantic convoys, *The Cruel Sea*, and when cinema goers could watch Humphrey Bogart and Katherine Hepburn in *The African Queen* or Ronald Reagan in *Bedtime for Bonzo* (a picture that would generate much greater interest thirty years later when Reagan became president of the United States).

Television was still something of a novelty, especially on this side of the Atlantic, and would only really begin to take off with the coronation of Elizabeth II two years later. Pop culture, manned space flight and mobile phones were all things of the future.

1

The early 1950s were not just a different world but a much more austere one too. Rationing was still in force (World War Two had ended just six years earlier) and life was hard. The affluent society had not yet arrived.

Perhaps in no sphere of life in 1951 was the contrast with our own time more marked than in the world of football. One of the characteristics of modern-day British football is that club chairmen or owners seem to be better known than the respective managers, the name of Roman Abramovich springing to mind.

Why should this be so? The answer is of course simple – money. When I first started to follow football – in the late 1960s and early 1970s – it was easy to name the manager and first-eleven line-up of all the First Division teams because managers and players tended to be loyal to their clubs. Appearance records set in these decades are unlikely ever to be broken.

Today there is so much money available that players are continually on the move, amassing fortunes undreamed of fifty years ago, and the game, I believe, has suffered as a consequence. Many footballers now seem to play purely for the financial rewards and as a result football has become not so much showbiz as a celebrity circus. How good a player someone is seems to matter less than the fabulous lifestyle exhibited in the newspapers and on television. In his autobiography, Derek Dougan, a novice professional at the 1958 World Cup, said of money and football:

> When a young player comes into the game interested in only what he can get out of it financially he misses the thrills that will sustain him in his dotage, when memory, as John Buchan said, holds the door. Neither will he know the meaning of team spirit, without which no progress is possible.[1]

Things were different in 1951. When Peter Doherty was appointed manager of Northern Ireland, football was still a sport, pure and simple; the game was played not because it led to riches untold – it didn't – but because it was loved. True, playing football was a better life than working down a coalmine or labouring on a building site but the wage differentials were not what they are now.

In his fascinating account of the varying fortunes brought by professional football to one family – the Summerbees – over three generations, entitled *Fathers, Sons and Football*, Colin Schindler paints a vivid picture of life for a player in the pre-celebrity, pre-television age. When Mike Summerbee began his career at Swindon Town in 1958, the year of the World Cup, club wages alone were insufficient to survive on:

> For some players, any spare time was spent on their second jobs – old pros Arnold Darcy and Pete Chamberlain were painters and decorators. After training and during the summer they donned the white overalls, strapped the ladders on to the roof of the little van and off they went – just like Beckham and Keane still do. Keith Morgan worked on building sites; Jack Smith and Cliff Jackson worked in the Wills cigarette factory, within sight of the County Ground. A summer job was imperative for both Mike and his new best friend Ernie Hunt ... Down the years Mike and Ernie's jobs got more exotic. One summer it was cutting the grass verges for the council, the next year it was digging graves. 'We got paid extra for an eighteen footer,' Mike recalls somewhat ghoulishly.

Grave digging is hardly an image that we associate with professional football today, yet this anecdote is proof that while the game in the 1950s had much to recommend it as a career, money did not feature very high on the list. Although it was a profession, football in that bygone age was still more of a sport than a business.

It offered both players and spectators passion and excitement, tragedy and triumph, despair and joy. This is the world in which our story is set, one perfectly captured by JB Priestly in *The Good Companions* in his ruminations about the fictional Yorkshire team Bruddersford United and its faithful supporters:

> To say that these men paid their shillings to watch twenty-two hirelings kick a ball is merely to say that a violin is wood and catgut, that Hamlet is so much paper and ink. For a shilling the Bruddersford United AFC offered you Conflict and Art; it turned you into a critic, happy in your judgement of fine points, ready in a second to estimate the worth of a well-judged pass, a run down the touch line, a lightening shot, a clearance kick by back or goalkeeper; it turned you into a partisan, holding your breath when the ball came sailing into your own goalmouth, ecstatic when your forwards raced away towards the opposition goal, elated, downcast, bitter, triumphant by turns at the fortunes of your side, watching a ball shape Iliads and Odysseys for you, and, what is more, it turned you into a member of a new community, all brothers together for an hour and a half, for not only had you escaped from the clanking machinery of the lesser life, from work, wages, rent, doles, sick pay, insurance cards, nagging wives, ailing children, bad bosses, idle workmen, but you had escaped with most of your mates and your neighbours, with half the town, and there you were, cheering together, thumping one another on the shoulders, swopping judgements like lords of the earth, having pushed your way through a turnstile into another and altogether more splendid kind of life, hurtling with Conflict and yet passionate and beautiful in its Art.[3]

This then is not just a book about football: it is a book about a bygone age and about sporting achievement to quicken the pulse and gladden the heart.

1. Derek Dougan, *Attack: The Autobiography of Derek Dougan*, Pelham Books, London, 1969, p. 135.

The squad was based in Tylösand and played their matches in Halmstad, Malmö and Norrköping. The final between Brazil and Sweden was in Stockholm with the third-place match between France and West Germany in Göteborg.

PROLOGUE

The match was in the second half and finely poised – Sweden 1, Brazil 2. The South Americans had been hot favourites to win the 1958 World Cup final but the host nation had stung them as early as the fourth minute, Liedholm putting the Swedes 1-0 up. That shock seemed to be exactly what a lethargic Brazil needed, and once Garrincha got into his stride on the right wing, Vavá scored twice to give the Brazilians a 2-1 half-time lead.

However, with only one goal separating the sides, and the home fans urging on the Swedish team, the game hung in the balance as the minutes ticked away. Then Nilton Santos, the powerhouse in the Brazil midfield, sent a high cross into Sweden's penalty area where the young Brazilian inside-left took charge of the ball, as he recalls:

> I stopped it on my thigh, kicked it in the air, whirled, and kicked it towards the goal as it came down. Svennson made a valiant effort to block the ball but it was to his left and it happened too fast for him to adjust. He was stretched out on the ground, his arms outstretched, as the ball went into the net.[1]

Pelé had just scored the decisive goal.

This was one of the most memorable incidents, if not the most memorable incident, of the 1958 World Cup, when one of the biggest footballing nations at last fulfilled its potential.

But this story is concerned with the smallest footballing nation in the 1958 World Cup, a tale no less dramatic and one that will evoke memories every bit as indelible as those of the seventeen-year-old boy wonder from Brazil. It begins seven years before Pelé walked onto the pitch at the Solna Stadium in Stockholm.

1. Pelé, *My Life and the Beautiful Game*, New English Library, 1977, p. 52.

ONE

DOHERTY
AND
BLANCHFLOWER

The first step taken by Northern Ireland on the road to the World Cup finals in Sweden '58 can be easily identified. It was taken on Tuesday, 27 September 1951 when the Irish Football Association's selection committee appointed a manager for the international team.

In the early 1950s the idea of giving one man responsibility for running an international side was still something of an innovation, though it did seem to point the way to the future for British international football: England's manager Walter Winterbottom was beginning his sixth season as manager in 1951–52. In fact Northern Ireland had had a manager before – Alf Peachey, who had doubled as manager of Distillery and under whom Northern Ireland had last won, prior to the decision taken in September 1951, when Scotland were beaten 2-0 on 6 October 1947. That statistic spoke for itself: four years without an international victory during which time team affairs were handled by a panel of selectors, part-time football administrators whose full-time occupation was more likely to be in some branch of business. 'It was unbelievable,' remarks Billy Bingham, 'that those people, who had never played, never managed, were in charge of selection.'

Indeed, team selection was erratic, as one bad result followed another, while match preparation lay somewhere between rudimentary and non-existent. When Danny

Blanchflower was first called up for international duty, against Scotland at Windsor Park in October 1949, his dreams about the glamour and professionalism of international-class football were quickly dissolved when he joined his colleagues at the seaside resort of Bangor:

> There we spent the mornings training, the afternoons wandering round the little shops or entrenched in the hotel lounge looking out over the October grey wastes of the Irish sea, the evenings at the local cinemas.
>
> The training stints were a shambles.
>
> 'You know what you want yourselves,' Gerry Morgan, the trainer, said to us as we donned the borrowed kit in the small dressing-room of the local team, 'if you don't know now you never will.'
>
> We trotted round the pitch for fifteen or twenty minutes and then grouped round one goalmouth, kicking a ball in turn at the goalkeeper.
>
> 'How about a five-a-side game?' somebody suggested.
>
> 'We don't want any injuries, Gerry,' one of the two officials with the party shouted; and that knocked on the head any idea we had of a bit of action.
>
> Afterwards we were all cheerful enough. We were international players and fit enough because we did regular training at our own clubs. We had not prepared much for an international match – but who cared? Nobody had done much, nobody had been hurt and nobody was responsible.[1]

Scotland won 8-2.

Blanchflower was not available for selection, due to injury, for the game against England at Maine Road, Manchester, the following month. The broken bone in his foot was a blessing in disguise. England went one better than the Scots, running out as embarrassingly easy 9-2 winners.

These two crushing defeats were part of a depressing post-war record for Northern Ireland up to the decision in September 1951 to put a manager in charge. Since the end of the war the team had played sixteen games, of which only two were won, while four were drawn and ten were lost. They had scored twenty-one goals but had conceded fifty-four, an average of more than three per game. As Danny Blanchflower summed up: 'There was no plan, no policy, no encouragement and very little hope.'[2] It was obviously time for a change.

The man to whom the IFA turned was currently the player-manager of Doncaster Rovers, but this was no journeyman lower-division footballer but rather the man football legend Stanley Matthews described as 'one of the greatest inside-forwards'[3] – Peter Doherty. Doherty was himself a legend, a hero to boys such as the young Danny Blanchflower growing up in east Belfast in the 1930s and who recalled vying with other youngsters in street matches for the right 'to be Peter Doherty'.[4] Doherty's international playing career had ended just as Blanchflower's was starting but they did play together once, against Scotland at Hampden Park in November 1950, in what proved to be Doherty's last appearance in the team. It was only his sixteenth cap for Northern Ireland, a fact that can be explained by the disruption to his playing career caused by World War Two and the decision of a number of IFA selection panels to omit him because he was too good and would therefore be a disruptive influence on the team. The only comment that seems appropriate is to imagine Brazil not playing Pelé in the 1970 World Cup finals.

Nonetheless, we have here an indication of the stature of Peter Doherty as a footballer and hence a need to put his appointment in the wider context of his career up to that point.

Doherty was born on 6 June 1913 in Magherafelt, County Londonderry, into a large family – six boys and three girls.

He attended St Malachy's elementary school in Coleraine where there was no school team and no properly organised games until he was in his teens. In fact, the young Doherty never even owned a pair of football boots – the only ones he ever wore were those provided by the clubs for which he played. But he loved football no matter what form it might take. When sent on errands he would often run with a tennis ball, hitting it against the wall and collecting the rebound, at the same time sharpening and perfecting his ball control.

His move into organised football came in season 1929–30 when he joined the junior side Station United, managed by Heedy Brown. Brown became an early mentor for Doherty whose innate talent he recognised and was careful to nurse and nurture. However, as much as he enjoyed the football, Station United did not offer paid employment and it was around the same time that Doherty's father got him a job as an apprentice builder on 7s per week.

Peter Doherty was never meant to be a builder – his light frame was not cut out for such heavy work and he was forced to give up after a few months. His next job was much more congenial, working as a conductor for his Uncle Peter's bus company which operated a local service between Coleraine and Portstewart.

Furthermore, he was able to fit his work around his football. Station United played at Victoria Park in Coleraine and on a Saturday afternoon he would get dropped off there, play a game, and then be picked up afterwards by the bus on the return leg to Portstewart and resume collecting fares. It was too good to last – and it didn't. Doherty's uncle was obliged to release young Peter from his employment when he discovered that his nephew was below the legal age to act as a conductor.

Doherty was out of work and understandably depressed. It was only his football that relieved the gloom and it was to be football that was to offer him a lifeline to a new start.

As a footballer he was beginning to attract attention, his all-action, thrusting style, starting and finishing attacks from the inside-forward position, marking him out as a special talent, as Malcolm Brodie, the *Belfast Telegraph* football reporter, was later to recall:

> Remember how he ran all over the field with an energy that amazed us all? Remember the brilliance of his footwork, passing, flair for anticipating the run of the ball and how he could suddenly stop and change direction? Remember those flashing legs and that peculiar loose-limbed style?[5]

Glentoran obviously were enamoured of the 'loose-limbed style' and offered Doherty a contract in 1931 – a signing-on fee of £24 and a weekly wage of £2 10s. The club also undertook to find Doherty a trade to follow in Belfast but did not in fact do so, leaving the eighteen-year-old with no regular income during the summer. That, however, was probably a small price to pay for regular Irish League football and the opportunity to showcase himself to the big English and Scottish professional clubs.

During his time with the Glens, Doherty picked up an Irish Cup winner's medal, scoring a goal in the 3-1 victory over Distillery at Windsor Park despite carrying an injury. He quickly established himself as one of the stars in the local game and it came as no surprise when after just two seasons at the Oval an offer came to take him into English football.

In November 1933 Doherty was transferred to Blackpool for £2,000. The Bloomfield Road club were a Second Division side but one of the better ones, with a realistic prospect of promotion. Again Doherty was to spend two seasons here as he had with Glentoran, in the process winning his first international cap, against England at Goodison Park in February 1935. A second cap was won in the same year, against Wales, but neither game provided memories to be cherished. Instead, Doherty experienced at first hand the problems he would try to address when he became the team's manager sixteen years later:

> There was a complete lack of cohesion about the Irish team in both these games. It was a collection of individuals, each striving to play well, regardless of the performance of the team as a whole. Team spirit was almost non-existent. We were a collection of units, hastily summoned together, and as such we played.[6]

He might have added 'and lost' (2-1 to England and 3-1 to Wales). Nonetheless, Doherty's prospects were looking up for in early 1936 he really entered the big time when Blackpool, short of money, were forced to sell their prize asset for £10,000 to First Division Manchester City.

That first season with City was unspectacular – ending in a very average ninth place, with forty-two points from forty-two games – but season 1936–37 was to see Manchester City crowned League champions for the first time, Doherty playing a key role and ending as top scorer with thirty league goals. In a pointer to the future, Doherty was later to remark on one vital quality that helped Manchester City outpace their rivals – team spirit:

> It is a mysterious and elusive thing; but once it has entered into a team it does not desert you if there is good feeling, comradeship and unselfishness among the players. I don't know which of these is the cardinal virtue; it doesn't really matter. We certainly had all three of them at Maine Road.[7]

Doherty's philosophy would ensure that all three would also be nurtured in the Northern Ireland side twenty years later.

Like so many others, World War Two robbed Doherty of his prime as a footballer but he was still a force to be reckoned with in 1945–46 when he won the FA Cup with Derby County, scoring one of the goals in the final against Charlton Athletic, just short of his thirty-third birthday.

In 1946 he moved to First Division strugglers Huddersfield Town for a transfer fee of £10,000 and it was at Leeds Road that he had his first taste of football management as player-manager. He was to help Huddersfield escape relegation before he moved on to Doncaster Rovers, again as player-manager. Under Doherty's guidance, Rovers won the Third Division (North) title and promotion to Division Two in 1949–50.

These forays into the management side of football revealed a new side to Peter Doherty: as someone with his own ideas about how teams should be run and players developed. He was ahead of his time with regards to training methods and in particular his advocacy of doing much more work with the ball, remarking:

> Some club managements believe that too much ball practice makes a player stale. It would be difficult to conceive a more stupid or erroneous idea. Every player, no matter how brilliant he is, has something to learn about ball control; and he can only overcome his difficulties by practising with the ball itself. This all-important aspect of training receives far too little attention in the weekly routine. Ball practice should figure prominently and often in all training schemes.[8]

Doherty was clearly a thinker about the game, a fact brought directly to the attention of his future employers, the IFA, shortly after World War Two. The governing body of association football in Northern Ireland was presented with a proposed coaching scheme by their star player, a blueprint for the future that must have impressed if not awed them. In summary, Doherty envisaged the establishment of a series of 'soccer centres' across Northern Ireland, but close to Irish League clubs, to be funded in partnership by the IFA, the clubs and individual subscriptions. Here boys of all ages would receive football training from suitably qualified coaches, following a set football curriculum. Although the IFA in the end turned the scheme down due to its expense, Doherty had shown that he was more than just a great player, in fact someone with a vision of how the game should be played and managed. He was a man who could play the game but also had ideas about how others could be taught to do the same. The coaching proposal was in a way Doherty's calling card with the IFA, and the response would come a few years later.

Around the same time that Doherty had drafted the proposal for the development of youth football, he had also completed writing his autobiography, published in 1947. In the conclusion in which he expounded his views on the role of the football manager, he wrote what amounted to his own job description for the post that would be offered to him four years later:

> Good managers, who are worth their often considerable weight in gold, are few and very far between ... Managership is a far from easy job. It entails a great deal of responsibility, and, besides an extensive knowledge of the game itself, a smattering of psychology is a desirable asset. Dealing with players' problems requires something besides football experience and business acumen. It demands understanding, and a sympathetic readiness to help at all times ... Football cannot afford to rest on its laurels. It must march abreast of the times, carrying its great record of the past into a still greater future.[9]

Of course Northern Ireland in 1951 did not have a 'great record of the past', a fact that had both advantages and disadvantages from Doherty's perspective. On the debit side there was no foundation of success on which to build; from a positive point of view, that very lack of success gave Doherty justification for radically changing the way the international side was run. Although the panel of selectors was officially to remain in place, the IFA can have been under no illusions, in the light of their own prior dealings with Doherty and the views he had quite publicly expressed, that the new manager would exploit to its fullest potential his remit to advise the panel on team selection and prepare the team for matches.

Doherty's baptism as team manager on 6 October 1951 was not especially encouraging – a 3-0 home defeat by Scotland – but soon enough he began to make his presence felt. Arguably the success that was to come Northern Ireland's way under Doherty comprised four main elements: the first of these was that quality which he had identified as the lynchpin of Manchester City's championship victory in 1936–37 – team spirit. Albert Sewell, who covered Northern Ireland in Sweden for the Associated Press, described Doherty as 'a magician as well as a manager' and said that there was 'no one in football better able to extract complete, constant endeavour from the men under his command'.[10]

Harry Gregg, who witnessed the twilight of Doherty's playing days at Doncaster, and described him as 'the greatest player that I have seen in my lifetime', recalls that 'his passion for the game was incredible ... he lived for it', telling his charges to 'chase a bad ball until you make it a good ball'. Gregg's fellow goalkeeper, Norman Uprichard, agrees wholeheartedly that Doherty was 'the greatest'. Quite simply Doherty was an inspiring leader and the transformation was particularly marked for those players like Danny Blanchflower who had experienced the ancien régime:

... through him [Doherty] the team found unity and identity. He brought an understanding, a vitality and a leadership to the players that had been sadly lacking before. Almost overnight he transformed the spirit of the team. We had a tremendous respect for him; and with his burning enthusiasm he urged us all to the extremes of our ability.[11]

Peter McParland would argue that it was more than respect that the players felt for this manager: 'The thing about it is, if you go through the whole Irish team ... they all idolised Peter Doherty.' It is an opinion echoed by Jimmy McIlroy, who has a vivid recollection of seeing 'Peter the Great' in action: 'I remember standing behind the goals at Windsor Park, it must have been as a fourteen-year-old, and seeing this [player] – he had like golden hair at that time – and everything he seemed to do was magical.' McIlroy, one of the fine talents to emerge in the 1950s, was equally impressed by Doherty as manager:

Half-an-hour's talk from manager Doherty could make eleven footballers go out and give their lives for Ireland. I have seen experienced stars like [Harry] Gregg and Jackie Blanchflower, their eyes transfixed on the boss, counting the minutes before they can run down the players' tunnel to get to grips with the enemy team.[12]

To emphasise the point, McIlroy now adds that 'if Peter had given us knives [or] daggers and told us "Knife these fellows as soon as you get out there [on the pitch]," we'd have done it'. When he compares Doherty to the other managers he played under during his career, McIlroy concludes, 'None of them ever inspired me like Peter Doherty did, and I think his team talks and his honesty had a terrific impact on the side.' And like Harry Gregg,

Jimmy McIlroy could not but be inspired by the manager's passion for the game:

> The thing that struck me first about him when I joined the Irish team – he was in his forties then, and he would join in [in] the seven-a-side [games] and I couldn't believe the effort and the running that he did ... It struck me then what a big heart, what an enthusiastic player this man must have been ... Peter, rightly or wrongly, expected this from every player.

'He was inspirational,' enthuses Billy Bingham, 'inspirational in his talks ... It was as if he was playing himself ... Peter Doherty was hands-on. Peter Doherty was with you all the time.' Moreover, Doherty did not need to intimidate to lead his charges. Although, as Bingham recalls, Doherty's sheer enthusiasm might have led him to salivate at the mouth when giving a team talk, Harry Gregg makes the point that 'he was a man who never raised his voice. He never shouted at people. He never was aggressive.' Presumably, he didn't throw hair dryers either – though, admittedly, such items would have been rare in a 1950s changing room.

Yet, at the same time, Doherty could relate to his players on their level; he could be, as Norman Uprichard puts it, 'just one of the boys'. Billy Bingham takes this point further, arguing that Doherty's success as a manager owed much to his achievements as a player:

> It does help if you've played the game at a high level; well, I think that, anyway. People say that you don't have to play at the highest level and there are managers who have been very successful [who haven't played at the top level] because they're organising a team, but you get probably more respect and they'll listen to you more [if

you had]. Because some players are very single-minded
and they think what they're doing's right ...

The second element of success in the Doherty era
was stability. The new manager was all too aware of the
negative impact frequent changes in personnel had on team
performances, writing of his own experience: 'Ireland's team
never seem to get an opportunity to settle like England's.
They are continually being changed, with the result that
players are unable to develop a thorough understanding
with each other.' Indeed it was a valid criticism of the set-up
prior to September 1951 that the Northern Ireland players
often knew their English, Scottish or Welsh opponents better
than they did each other. Players were often chosen by the
selectors for what Harry Gregg describes as 'geographic
reasons', so that the team would be truly representative of
the province.

Such logic might make sense when it comes to an
American presidential candidate choosing a running-mate
for the election, but it was a bizarre approach to picking a
national football team. Now under Doherty the side began
to assume a settled appearance and the players got to know
each other. A virtue was made out of a necessity in that
Northern Ireland had a much more limited pool of players to
select from than say England or Scotland but Doherty soon
identified his best team and got it functioning almost like
a club side in the international arena. They soon became a
tightly-knit group whose cohesion and spirit was probably
better than any other nation.

To spirit and stability Doherty added organisation. No
longer were there the aimless running and kick-abouts
Danny Blanchflower had had to endure in the run-up to
his first international appearance: a thoroughly professional
approach was now adopted and soon became a hallmark of
Doherty's international sides. Writing in 1957, Jack Milligan

of the *Daily Mirror* remarked on how the gap in class between Northern Ireland and the rest of the UK footballing nations had narrowed significantly, drawing a contrast with the pre-Doherty period:

> Things are different now. The Irish team is a well-organised unit. Each man knows what he is supposed to do ... Doherty gets the best out of every man. And what is more important – the players respect his advice, welcome his discipline and are always ready to pull out that little bit extra for the boss who is one of the boys.[13]

The last comment is significant as it is indicative of the fact that Doherty always sought to strike a balance between having his teams thoroughly prepared and encouraging the players to enjoy the experience. The team always had a sense of fun, again reflecting its closer assimilation to a club side than a conventional international side, and its secret weapon in keeping the mood light and cheerful was trainer Gerry Morgan. It was Morgan who was believed to be the originator of the much quoted tactic that Northern Ireland should always aim to equalise before the opposition scored.

Spirit, stability and organisation made Northern Ireland a much more formidable team than they had been in the immediate post-war period but they would still not have won many games without the fourth ingredient added to the mix by Doherty – a sense of adventure. Doherty had been an attacking player and he was to be an attacking manager. This was like a breath of fresh air to supporters who had so long been stifled by negative tactics; it was an absolute joy to attack-minded players like Jimmy McIlroy:

> Caution was forgotten as wing-halves and even full-backs were told to go out and enjoy their football, and even score a few goals if the fancy took them. The wearers of

green, filled with the spirit of adventure, became, with one throw of the dice, an attacking team, an attractive team, and a successful team.[14]

As Peter McParland adds, 'The great thing about him was he kept everything simple.' Even the England manager of this era, Walter Winterbottom, in a somewhat backhanded compliment, recognised Doherty's precious gift to his team:

Peter was just a player who moved into management. He had no knowledge of the sports sciences or coaching or motivation [!] except that he was looked up to because of his own ability. Like all players of that ability, he struck a chord, a rapport with those under him who wanted to play like he did, and he was willing to let his team play football.[15]

That freedom to let the team express itself or, as Winterbottom put it, 'play football', would have counted for very little had not Northern Ireland in the course of the Doherty revolution been blessed with a crop of players with talent to express. Among that group, one player in particular stood out, not just because of his skill on the pitch but because he too was a thinker on the game. This was the man who would become captain and as it were Peter Doherty's right-hand man, producing a partnership that was to take Northern Ireland football to heights undreamed.

The captain of a football team in the 1930s was more akin to an assistant manager in modern football than to the man who wears the distinguishing armband in the current game. Therefore the choice of a skipper for the Northern Ireland team was not something Peter Doherty was going to take lightly. He obviously wanted an outstanding footballer but something more than that as well: a player who would command respect and have a knowledge of the game to allow him to respond tactically to developments during the course of a match; a man who could take over if necessary from his manager when the opening whistle sounded (remember that this was in the days before substitutes were allowed). To the great good fortune of both Doherty and Northern Ireland a candidate for the post was waiting in the wings.

Danny Blanchflower, the youngster who had idolised Doherty in the 1930s, was an extraordinary talent from a very ordinary background. Born on 10 February 1926 (making him thirteen years Doherty's junior) in Bloomfield in east Belfast, Blanchflower's was an archetypal working-class upbringing. His father, John, was a shipyard worker while his mother in her spare time played inside-forward for the local women's team, this in an era when women's football was a real novelty. Blanchflower certainly did not feel his childhood was a deprived one, though his later recollection almost verges on the idyllic:

> But for me, Belfast was the streets in which I played football ... the little school within easy reach ... the chip-shop round the corner where we hacked out the big slide during the cold frosty weather ... the old night-watchman's hut and the glowing coke brazier that we snuggled around and vied with one another in telling ghost stories until we were all too scared to go home in the dark ... the 'wee hall' nearby where early on Saturday nights they showed the silent movies and we shrieked our heads off, warning the hero to 'look behind you' as the villain sneaked up; or to 'hurry up' as he dashed to save the beautiful girl from the terrible fate that we had seen and he hadn't ...[16]

The 'little school' was Ravenscroft elementary, a somewhat dilapidated structure that nonetheless had the virtue of not having overcrowded classes. Here, at break and lunch and when lessons were over for the day, the main pastime was playing football. In winter, games might even continue after dark, 'floodlit' by the street lamps.

Blanchflower's first experience of organised team play was with the 19th Belfast Wolf Cub XI, where Billy Maxwell was in charge. In his first match Blanchflower scored three goals and by the age of ten was turning out regularly for both his school team (on Saturday morning) and for the cubs (on Saturday afternoon). When he became too old to play for the cubs he moved on to the Boys Brigade primarily because they had a football team, thus continuing to play two matches on a Saturday. Football was to be a constant in Blanchflower's life, no matter how circumstances might change, and when he won a scholarship to the Belfast College of Technology (now the Belfast Metropolitan College) he also secured a place in the college's team at inside-right.

Blanchflower had academic ability and the college offered him the chance of taking an exam to gain entrance to university; however, the harsh reality of life was that he was expected by the family to learn a trade and start bringing money into the home. An uncle secured a place for him as an apprentice electrician at Gallahers, the cigarette manufacturers, and so his future seemed to be mapped out.

But war had broken out in September 1939 and it was to alter Blanchflower's course as it did that of countless others. His father had joined the army and now Danny enrolled as a cycle messenger with the ARP (Air Raid Precaution Service). He still played football when he could and even started up his own team, Bloomfield United. It was at this stage that he came to the notice of the senior team in east Belfast, Glentoran, for whom he signed as an amateur and still short of his sixteenth birthday. At the Oval he found himself on the fringes of the team but it was undoubtedly a step up for an aspiring footballer.

As the war raged on, Blanchflower now joined the Air Training Corps and from there graduated to the RAF as a trainee navigator. He also had the opportunity to study at St Andrew's University in Scotland for one year before commencing aircrew training proper. Blanchflower relished the university experience, a pleasure perhaps intensified because it had been delayed. He studied maths, physics and applied kinematics but seemed to appreciate every aspect of the academic environment:

> The town, surrounded on three sides by the sea, retains an old-world charm about it that fosters better the feeling of that measured concept of life. And being exposed to it had a deep and lasting impression on me ... the wearing of the scarlet gown, the adult approach and pursuit of knowledge ...[17]

Blanchflower was clearly a thinker as well as a player, just like Peter Doherty, but he came back down to earth, as it were, when he entered full-time RAF training. He was stationed first in Torquay and then at a number of Midlands' camps before being moved to Canada. He was scheduled for departure to the Far East when Japan surrendered and hence was sent back to England. He now had plenty of opportunity to play football with his fellow RAF trainees who included the future actor Richard Burton.

Blanchflower returned to Belfast for Christmas leave in 1945 and turned out for Glentoran reserves. His game had now developed and so impressed were the Glens' management that he was promoted to the first team for the game against Belfast Celtic and then offered a contract as a part-time professional. Blanchflower must have found it difficult to keep up with the pace of developments but he now faced a hard decision, still having the option, as he did, to complete his study at St Andrew's. In the end he was persuaded by

Glens manager George Thompson and director Bob Harpur that he was being offered a very good deal (a signing-on fee of £50 and then £3 per match) and so he signed on the dotted line.

In April 1946 Blanchflower was released from the RAF and returned to Belfast to complete his apprenticeship at Gallahers before commencing life as a part-time professional footballer. During the incoming season (1946–47) Blanchflower made the breakthrough into regular first-team football, now settling into the position he would make his own, right-half. In February 1947 he won his first representative honour when he was chosen to play for the Irish League against the English League at Goodison Park, but, like Doherty, his football destiny lay in the English League and when an offer came in to take him to Second Division Barnsley in April 1949, he grabbed it with both hands. The transfer fee was £6,000.

In his first full season in English football, Blanchflower made his international debut, that eminently forgettable affair against Scotland referred to earlier. One common factor between that event and what he now routinely experienced with Barnsley was the lack of imagination in the training methods employed and the noted absence of the ball. He wrote later about his time at Oakwell:

> This was my second year of full-time training and it was beginning to seem a grim monotonous grind to me ... Perhaps there is something in the British make-up that compels the idea that a man must go through hell and high water to get anywhere. It doesn't seem to matter whether he is going in the right direction or not – so long as he is suffering, then everything should be all right ... In those pre-season training days there was little attention paid to training with the ball. Playing with the ball was something we enjoyed: and enjoying something was out

– or so it seemed … The result was that we finished fit and strong enough – but it was a condition estranged from good football simply because we had neglected to match the advancing degrees of skill and speed with the ball, with the advancing degree of our physical fitness.[18]

Blanchflower simply could not endure such a regime and was sure enough of himself to vocalise his concerns with the powers that be. The exchange of opinions with Barnsley manager Angus Seed now seems hardly credible, Blanchflower appealing for greater access to the ball to sharpen his skills:

'I don't believe in that sort of practice,' he said. 'If you don't see the ball during the week you'll be more keen to get it on Saturdays.'
I was amazed. 'But if I don't get some practice I won't know what to do with it when I do get in on Saturdays,' I replied.
He ordered me out of his office.[19]

Like Peter Doherty, Danny Blanchflower wanted to play football and to do that you needed a ball. Obviously Barnsley were not yet ready to accommodate such a revolutionary idea. For Blanchflower it was time to move on and up. In March 1951, just six months before Doherty was named as Northern Ireland manager, the twenty-five-year-old right-half was transferred to First Division Aston Villa for a fee of £15,000.

Blanchflower was now in the class of football where he belonged. Never one of the quickest players, he more than made up for this deficiency with his measured passing and attuned reading of the game. When given full rein, as he was eventually at Tottenham Hotspur, he could best be compared to a great conductor leading an orchestra – when Blanchflower played well so did his team. In this respect he was a born

27

leader who coaxed others with his deft skills and who could get in the fray and tackle hard when it was needed. He left a lasting impression on the young Terry Venables who aspired to play in the same right-half position:

> He combined graceful movements with remarkable skill. His game was about subtlety and speed of thought, about awareness and perception that allowed interception before confrontation – although he defended well when the occasion demanded. I think the perfection of Danny's passing will always remain as a vivid memory. His best pass was hit from the right side of midfield, lofted 35 yards into the inside-left position. It posed a constant threat to the opposition.[20]

Blanchflower's arrival at Villa Park signalled a revival by the Birmingham club which had seemed certain to be relegated but now ended the season a comfortable fifteenth. During Blanchflower's three full seasons with Villa they would in fact never finish in as low a position again. In terms of international football, too, the prospects were encouraging. The new Northern Ireland manager quickly recognised in Blanchflower a kindred spirit and a player of the type of stature and talent around which a team could be built, as John Camkin, of the *Daily Mail*, observed:

> Doherty, one of the greatest of modern British inside-forwards, created a plan of constructive football based on right-half Danny Blanchflower ... He exploited to the utmost the powerful attacking method which had made Blanchflower one of the outstanding half-backs in world football.

Blanchflower now became a permanent fixture in the Northern Ireland team; indeed from the game against Wales in March 1952 he would not miss a match until the encounter with Italy in April 1961 (his final tally of caps would be fifty-six). Furthermore, Doherty saw Blanchflower as an extension of himself on the pitch, someone who could take on the role of leader when a game got underway. Blanchflower was first given the captaincy during Northern Ireland's tour of Canada at the end of the 1952–53 season, the match against Manitoba in Winnipeg. That game sealed the partnership between two of the most creative men in football; certainly Blanchflower had advanced views on the role he had now been assigned:

> ... I was determined to be more than just a captain in name only. I wanted to face the demands of the position, to challenge its problems and act upon my decisions: better to learn from experience than to do nothing ... a good captain can help a team along by good decisions. You cannot define captaincy or reduce it to fixed conceptions: it is a complex business, an art, an eternal improvisation. It is a battle of wits and you can never be sure.[21]

Blanchflower's views on captaincy were somewhat too advanced for his future Spurs manager Jimmy Anderson who took the captaincy away from his talented right-half on the grounds that he had exceeded his authority. Specifically Anderson was aggrieved by changes Blanchflower had made to the team in a couple of matches, the Northern Ireland star countering with the argument that these had been exceptional circumstances when he felt he had to gamble to try to win games Spurs had been losing. Certainly no such friction ever seemed to affect his relationship with Doherty as the players were quick to testify, Peter McParland speaking of 'a team inspired by the off-field magic of manager Doherty and the on-field example of Danny Blanchflower'.[22] Under a different manager at Tottenham – Bill Nicholson – the Northern Ireland captain was given the freedom to express his leadership potential in a similar fashion to his role under Doherty, Terry Venables noting:

> Danny was nominally the club's captain, but he enjoyed significantly more influence over the team than is normally the case. He was virtually the manager on the field. Spurs' actual manager, Bill Nicholson, allowed Danny his free run so that his undoubted leadership qualities could be exploited fully … On the pitch Danny was free to make changes as he saw fit, as the state of the game demanded. The players all recognised his leadership qualities and responded to his commands without any dissension … I have seen players take on this role – Michel Platini [former captain of France] is an example – but it has to be a very special relationship between player and manager …[23]

It soon became clear to all concerned that such a bond existed between Peter Doherty and Danny Blanchflower. It was during the same Canadian tour in which Blanchflower first captained Northern Ireland that he and the manager had got together to discuss the fundamentals of how the game should be played, this after a defeat by fellow-visitors Switzerland in Montreal. The Swiss had confounded Northern Ireland by not adhering to the conventional British formation of play, the 2-3-5 system (two full-backs, three half-backs and five forwards, the inside-forwards acting as links between defence and attack) and this stimulated both Doherty and Blanchflower into reassessing the shape a team could take on the field.

At one time, defeat had been just part of the routine for the international side but under Doherty, and influenced by Blanchflower, it became a lesson, an experience on which to build. Blanchflower was an early advocate of studying the football style of the continentals (1953 also being the year in which Hungary had humiliated England 6-3 at Wembley) and a proponent of a more flexible style of play, such as a 3-3-4 formation. In fact he almost got Aston Villa to adopt the experiment but was disappointed when the manager dropped the scheme after just one trial game. Peter Doherty, fortunately for Northern Ireland, had more imagination and a genuine commitment to challenging the football orthodoxies of the day. This fresh approach by manager and captain also manifested itself in the training strategy employed, as left-half Bertie Peacock remarked:

> Peter and Danny didn't have us running up and down sandhills, it was all about football. The two of them were before their time, everything they did was about method, about playing, passing the ball with intention rather than for its own sake. The main thing was that when they asked the players to do something, we could understand how and why we were going to do it.[24]

In Harry Gregg's opinion, 'Peter and Danny were made for each other.' A team talk in his recollection would consist of Doherty giving brief instructions and then asking the players to contribute, after which 'Danny would talk for the next two hours'. Peter McParland endorses that view: 'Danny had the gift of the gab ... he would do his bit for a fair old time.' Jimmy McIlroy remarks that Blanchflower 'really thought the world of Peter Doherty' and that 'so many times Peter agreed with Danny's idea[s]'. Not that they always saw eye to eye – Gregg recalls a team conversation on the eve of the match against England in November 1957 when Doherty said that if he found his good friend Tom Finney through on the Northern Ireland goal he would have no hesitation in bringing him down, to which Blanchflower objected as against the rules and spirit of the game. Jackie Blanchflower then interjected to say that the only reason his brother wouldn't commit a foul in these circumstances was because he was afraid his opponent might get up and hit him.

McParland also remembers Blanchflower as supportive and nurturing, especially to young players like himself when they played together for a time at English club football:

> He was a great captain, not only for Ireland but for Tottenham. I played with him at Villa [where] he was a terrific help to me. The first time I played I was a nineteen-year-old and he said, 'If you're ever in trouble, look up, I'll be there – knock it inside, I'm waiting to help you.'

Blanchflower's stature as both a player and captain was recognised when he was chosen by Walter Winterbottom, the England manager, to lead a Great Britain side against a European XI at Windsor Park in August 1955 in a game marking the seventy-fifth anniversary of the founding of the IFA. Three years later he was voted Player of the Year, an accolade he received again in 1961, at the end of the season in which he captained Tottenham Hotspur (whom he had joined in December 1954 from Villa) to the double – the first team in the twentieth century to win the League Championship and FA Cup in the same campaign.

Danny Blanchflower was one of the all-time greats, Dave Bowler, Blanchflower's biographer (and biographer of Bill Shankly and Sir Alf Ramsey), asserting that he was the best captain the British game has ever produced. Peter Doherty would not have argued with that assessment but both manager and captain would have acknowledged that the 1950s witnessed a flowering of football talent in Northern Ireland, the likes of which had never been seen before and arguably would not be repeated for another quarter century. The Great Britain select team that took on Europe at Windsor

Park in August 1955 included two other local players – Jimmy McIlroy and Bertie Peacock – but that was simply a pointer to the fact that under Peter Doherty a new Northern Ireland was beginning to emerge.

1. Danny Blanchflower, *The Double and Before ...*, Nicholas Kaye, 1961, pp 139–40.
2. Ibid., p. 144.
3. Peter Doherty, *Spotlight on Football*, Art and Educational Publishers, London, 1947, p. ix.
4. Blanchflower, p. 32.
5. N Ireland v. Scotland, Windsor Park, Belfast, 8 October 1955, official match programme.
6. Doherty, p. 89.
7. Ibid., p. 44.
8. Ibid., p. 109.
9. Ibid., p. 118.
10. John Camkin, *World Cup 1958*, The Sportsman's Book Club edition, 1959, p. 121.
11. Blanchflower, p. 145.
12. Jimmy McIlroy, *Right Inside Soccer*, The Sportsman's Book Club, 1961, p. 110.
13. N Ireland v. Portugal, Windsor Park, Belfast, 1 May 1957, official match programme.
14. McIlroy, p. 116.
15. Dave Bowler, *Danny Blanchflower: A Biography of a Visionary*, Victor Gollancz, 1997, p. 127.
16. Blanchflower, p. 5.
17. Ibid., p. 10.
18. Ibid., pp. 31–2.
19. Ibid., p. 35.
20. Terry Venables, *Terry Venables' Football Heroes*, Virgin Books, 2001, p. 28.
21. Blanchflower, pp. 171–3.
22. Peter McParland, *Going for Goal*, Souvenir Press Ltd, 1960, p. 26.
23. Venables, p. 30.
24. Bowler, pp. 125–6.

TWO

A TEAM OF (NEARLY) ALL THE TALENTS

Peter Doherty would have been the first to acknowledge that his tenure as manager of Northern Ireland coincided with the emergence of a set of players whose ability set them apart from earlier teams and indeed many of the international sides that would follow. For the first time in its history, Northern Ireland had, if not quite an embarrassment of riches, certainly a wealth of talent that would allow it to compete with, and often beat, the very best in the world. Gregg has described the make-up of the squad as a mixture of 'good players and great players', twelve or thirteen of whom he considers to have been Premier League class.

These players undoubtedly needed Peter Doherty to mould them into an effective unit, but equally it was the prodigious skills that they brought with them that made it possible for the manager to produce a team capable of making its mark in the World Cup. Doherty was the right man in the right place at the right time – Northern Ireland in the 1950s.

The goalkeeping position is the most critical on the football field. If you don't have a good goalkeeper, rarely will you have a good team (the Brazil side of 1970 being an exception, but then they were an exceptional team in so many ways). Good 'keepers can be an inspiration to their teams, leading as it were from the back: think of Gordon Banks for England (and what happened when he was missing against West Germany in the World Cup quarter-final in 1970); Ray Clemence for Liverpool and Peter Shilton for Nottingham Forest in the 1970s; Peter Schmeichel for Manchester United in the 1990s; and not forgetting Pat Jennings for Northern Ireland in the first half of the 1980s.

Peter Doherty was then fortunate to have two very fine 'keepers at his disposal: Norman Uprichard, a native of Lurgan, who as a child was taken to watch Glenavon 'on the bar of the bike' and who was transferred to Arsenal in June 1948; and Harry Gregg, a member of the 'Busby Babes' at Manchester United. Uprichard, or 'Black Jake' to his team-mates, was the regular custodian during the early part of the Doherty era, but even when he lost his first-choice status (initially because of injury) he remained an important member of the squad, before that term was commonly used. Indeed he would feature in crucial World Cup games in both the qualifying and final stages. Uprichard still regards pulling on the international 'keeper's jersey for the first time as the highlight of his career. But of the two men, Gregg was the one destined for distinction, through a combination of ability and circumstance.

Harry Gregg was born on 27 October 1932 in Tobermore, County Londonderry, the eldest of six children (five boys and one girl). The family later moved to Windsor Avenue in Coleraine where Gregg spent his teenage years and attended Coleraine Model School and the local Technical College.

Gregg's first job was as an apprentice joiner but his first love was always football. After playing for a number of junior teams in the Coleraine area, he was signed by Linfield. Gregg never made the first team at Windsor Park and was transferred, ironically, to his home town team of Coleraine, earning a weekly wage of £3 10s.

Gregg continued to work as a joiner but it was his performances on the football pitch that were about to transform his life, for he now came to the notice of Peter Doherty. Doherty, a former Coleraine player himself of course, combined the roles of Northern Ireland manager and manager of Second Division Doncaster Rovers and it was in the latter capacity that he offered Gregg the chance to move to full-time professional football in England. Although it meant taking a cut in pay (his combined weekly wage at home as a joiner and part-time footballer being £11 while at Doncaster he would earn only £7 in winter and £6 in summer), Gregg followed his star and signed for a transfer fee of £1,200 in October 1952 making his debut the following January at the age of twenty.

It was as a Doncaster Rovers player that Harry Gregg made his debut for Northern Ireland, against Wales at Wrexham in March 1954. It was an auspicious start, as team-mate Jimmy McIlroy recalled:

> This was the first time I had seen Harry Gregg, a master goalkeeper, in action. I thought he was brilliant, particularly as I feared the menace of John Charles, Britain's most expensive footballer, as leader of the Welsh attack.
> As centres came over, from either wing, Gregg performed like a cat, picking the ball off the head of Charles ... often as far out as the eighteen-yard-line.[1]

This British Championship match was also a World Cup qualifier and thanks in large part to Gregg's performance (and that of another debutant, Peter McParland, who scored twice) Northern Ireland won 2-1, recording their first victory in Wales since 1923.

Harry Gregg was clearly meant for the big time, and after ninety-three league games for Doncaster, the big time duly beckoned when in December 1957 Manchester United, the reigning League champions, paid out a then world record fee for a goalkeeper – £23,500 – to take the twenty-five-year-old to Old Trafford.

Gregg was worth every penny, going on to play in 210 league games for United between 1957–58 and 1966–67. However, despite his excellence on the field of play, he is probably best remembered at Old Trafford as one of the heroes of the Munich air crash in February 1958. At great personal risk he entered the wreckage of the plane to drag to safety a mother and baby (Verena and Vesna Lukic) and his team-mates Dennis Viollet and Bobby Charlton.

He also found and assisted his Northern Ireland colleague Jackie Blanchflower who was moaning in agony – across him lay the team's left-back, Roger Byrne, unmarked and with his eyes open but dead. All the while that Gregg was engaged in pulling others clear of the carnage, explosions were going off and at any moment he could have lost his life.

Harry Gregg was no ordinary goalkeeper, as his displays for club and country would prove (winning twenty-four caps) but he was no ordinary man either.

The full-back positions usually rotated between three players: Willie Cunningham, Alfie McMichael and Dick Keith. Cunningham was born in Mallusk, on the outskirts of Belfast, on 20 February 1930 but was brought up in Scotland. His first senior club was St Mirren and it was as a St Mirren player that he played his first game for Northern Ireland, against Wales in March 1951.

Cunningham was a versatile defender who could fill either full-back slot or perform competently at centre-half, but it was as a full-back that he was signed by Leicester City in December 1954. He would go on to make 127 league appearances for the Foxes, scoring four goals, up to the 1959–60 season.

Cunningham became Northern Ireland's first-choice right-back from November 1955 but when the Munich disaster in February 1958 deprived the team of the services of Jackie Blanchflower as centre-half, the Leicester player was switched to that position for all the upcoming games in Sweden.

Jackie Blanchflower's misfortune was Dick Keith's opportunity. The Newcastle United right-back had only made his international debut in 1957 against England and was very much the second choice after Willie Cunningham. But Cunningham's forced move to centre-half left the right-back berth free for Keith and he seized the moment, playing in all the games in Sweden and going on to win twenty-three caps for his country.

A Belfast lad, Dick Keith had played locally for Linfield before being transferred to Newcastle United in September 1956. In 208 league matches for the Geordies he scored two goals and later moved on to Bournemouth.

Northern Ireland's established left-back in this period was Alfie McMichael, whose career path was followed to an extraordinary degree by Dick Keith. Like Keith, whose senior he was by five years, McMichael was born in Belfast, played for Linfield and was transferred to Newcastle (in September 1949). He was at St James' Park throughout the glory Cup years of the 1950s, making 402 league appearances (one goal).

McMichael made his international debut the month after his transfer to English football, playing against Scotland, and became a permanent fixture in Peter Doherty's side, accumulating a total of forty caps. When Dick Keith established himself in the Northern Ireland side in 1958, a memorable club and country full-back partnership was born, one that would benefit the players and the teams for which they played.

Northern Ireland's half-back line was dominated by the vision and cultured passing of the man who made the right-half position his own, the captain Danny Blanchflower. Inevitably, by comparison those who occupied the centre-half and left-half positions appeared more journeymen players. In their own right, however, the men who performed those roles had a lot of ability and more importantly made a vital contribution to team play by providing the necessary hard edge to balance Blanchflower's finesse.

A half-back line had to have balance to be effective. The centre-half was always a defender, a 'stopper' of opposing forwards, but wing-halfs had to complement each other. If both the right-half and the left-half were tacklers, with the emphasis on negating the efforts of the opposition, then the team would lack creativity. Equally, if both wing-halfs were ball players, then the team would be weakened defensively.

The best and most successful teams in this era had one artist and one artisan in these roles, for example Eddie Coleman and Duncan Edwards at Manchester United. Spurs' great double-winning side of 1960–61 had the silky skills of Danny Blanchflower combined with the tough tackling of Dave Mackay. Blanchflower played a similar part for Northern Ireland with the left-half providing the bite to support his brilliance.

Wilbur Cush, Bertie Peacock and Tommy Casey are all illustrative of this point. Cush, born in Lurgan on 10 June 1928, and arguably the greatest footballer ever produced by the mid-Ulster town, played normally at wing-half or inside-forward but, when required, could also fill the centre-half position. Despite his short stature, Cush was not intimidated by taller opposing forwards.

What he lacked in inches he more than made up for with iron tackling and determination, his gritty displays an inspiration to those around him. Jim Storey, a follower of the international team in the Doherty years, remembers Wilbur Cush as 'a terrier', someone with a 'heart bigger than his body', while to Harry Gregg he is 'the most underrated player in the history of Irish football' who 'never got the credit he deserved'.

Playing his way up through the junior ranks with Carrick (winners of the Irish Schools Cup in 1941–42), 2nd Lurgan Boys Brigade, Lurgan Boys Club (winners of the Irish Junior Cup) and Shankill Young Men, Cush entered senior local football with hometown club Glenavon whom he helped become the first side from outside Belfast to win the Irish League championship. It was while he was with the Mourneview side that he made his international debut against Scotland in October 1953, the first of twenty-six Northern Ireland appearances.

In November 1957 Cush was transferred to Leeds United, for whom he would play eighty-nine league games and score nine goals, and it was as a tough-tackling Leeds player that he would represent Northern Ireland in the 1958 World Cup finals. Jimmy McIlroy, Cush's fellow inside-forward for most of those games, was well-placed to appreciate Wilbur's contribution to the team:

> Wilbur Cush was a pocket battleship ... the most underrated player that has ever pulled on an Irish jersey ... a superb all-round footballer ... Inside-forward, wing-half – you could have played him virtually anywhere on the field apart from goals ... and the only other player that I can say that about was Tom Finney ... I feel he never received the acclaim that he deserved.

Bertie Peacock could also tackle and this allied with his boundless energy earned him the nickname of the 'Little Ant'. Peacock's tireless displays at left-half for his country (and for his clubs Glentoran and Celtic, with whom he earned every Scottish football honour) were the perfect foil to the more measured game of Danny Blanchflower. Though as Billy Bingham observes, Peacock could also create:

He could change the ball from left-midfield to right wing, to me on the right wing. I knew if Bertie was looking at [Peter] McParland and McParland was getting covered [by the defence], Bertie would switch it – bang! – get the ball to the right wing. It was a move we just played naturally.

Peacock's first game for Northern Ireland was also Peter Doherty's first as manager – against Scotland in October 1951. Eleven years later it was Bertie Peacock who succeeded Doherty as manager.

For all his success in his position, Bertie Peacock did not go unchallenged for a place in the international side. Tommy Casey was always waiting in the wings – almost literally – for a chance to show what he could do. Casey, born in Comber on 11 March 1930, played Irish League football for Bangor before being transferred to Leeds in May 1949. His stay at Elland Road, however, was short and not very sweet. He made only four league appearances before falling out with manager Frank Buckley and returning to Northern Ireland.

He soon made his way back to English football with Bournemouth and after a couple of seasons joined the cup kings of the 1950s – Newcastle United – with whom he won an FA Cup winner's medal. Casey became part of a Northern Ireland trio at St James' Park, playing alongside Dick Keith and Alfie McMichael, but the World Cup season of 1957–58 was to be his last with Newcastle, moving to the opposite end of the country to finish his career at Portsmouth and Bristol City. The fact that he won only twelve caps for Northern Ireland is less a reflection on his ability than on that of his rival for the number six shirt, Bertie Peacock.

Twelve caps was also the final total achieved by centre-half Jackie Blanchflower, but this was entirely due to great misfortune. Jackie, who was born on 7 March 1933, was the younger brother of Danny and a member of the famous

Busby Babes side of the mid-1950s. He was 'discovered' by Manchester United's local talent-spotter Bob Harpur playing for Pitt Street Mission in the Belfast Boys Club League, and whisked off to Old Trafford in March 1950.

Between 1950–51 and 1957–58, Jackie Blanchflower played 105 league games for United and scored twenty-six league goals. He famously took over in goal from Ray Wood in the 1957 FA Cup final against Aston Villa, after Wood's collision with Blanchflower's fellow Ulsterman Peter McParland.

It was as a Busby Babe that Jackie joined his brother in the Northern Ireland side for the first time, against England in October 1954. His best game for his country came just over three years later in the game that clinched qualification for the 1958 World Cup finals. Within a few weeks of that memorable Windsor Park victory, Jackie Blanchflower lay amidst the wreckage of the aircraft carrying the Manchester United team at Munich. Blanchflower survived, thanks in great measure to the ministrations of his international colleague Harry Gregg, but his injuries – eight broken ribs, two fractures of the pelvis, and kidney damage – ruled him out of any further involvement in top-class football. A defender who could tackle and pass, 'a footballing centre-half' in the words of Harry Gregg, Jackie Blanchflower, like so many of his Manchester United team-mates, was struck down in his prime.

In general, Northern Ireland sides have tended to be characterised by competent and resolute defences but equally by much less inspiring attack formations. The team of the 1950s certainly had a good defence but with the positive approach of Peter Doherty and the blossoming of a new generation of creative and attacking talent, a forward line of some potential began to take shape.

On the right wing Billy Bingham established himself as a player of pace and power who could both create and score goals. Born on 5 August 1931 in the Bloomfield area of east Belfast (in the street adjoining that where the Blanchflowers grew up), Bingham was something of a football prodigy. He captained his school team (Elmgrove Elementary) to victory in the Ulster Schools Cup and represented Northern Ireland in wartime schools internationals.

At the age of sixteen, Bingham followed in his father's footsteps when he started work at the local Harland and Wolff shipyard, beginning an apprenticeship as an electrician. Football, however, remained his passion and around the same time he signed as an amateur for the team he had always followed – Glentoran. At the Oval he lined up in the third team alongside his near neighbour and childhood footballing playmate Jackie Blanchflower. That side also included a young inside-forward from Lambeg called Jimmy McIlroy whose star, like that of Bingham, was in the ascendant. Danny Blanchflower by this stage was a professional player for Glentoran, making the club something of a nursery for the international side of the 1950s. Indeed when Bingham was promoted to the Glens second team he found himself playing alongside another future international, Bertie Peacock.

In 1948 Bingham became a part-time professional on a weekly wage of £6 and was promoted to the first team along with McIlroy and Peacock. It was also in this period that he was switched from the centre-forward role he had been occupying to outside-right, which became his permanent position. The move obviously worked because two years later Sunderland made Glentoran an offer of £10,000 to take the nineteen-year-old to Roker Park.

Bingham received the news while he was in the bath at Bloomfield Road, Blackpool, after playing for the Irish League against the English League. Later that evening he met the Sunderland manager Bill Murray and heard that the clubs had already agreed terms, leaving the final decision up to the youngster. After talking to his parents back in Belfast, Bingham was on his way to English football. What he wasn't aware of at the time was that the man who had first told him about the approach by Sunderland, while he relaxed in the Blackpool bath, was none other than Charles Buchan, he of *Football Monthly* fame and a one-time star with the north-east club.

Bingham remembers arriving on Wearside and being 'taken in past the shipyards', to his mind 'a replica of Belfast'. Although he faced stiff competition for a place in the first team, he applied himself single-mindedly to the task, helped, he feels, by the extra work he had done while still at the Oval to develop his physique:

> Funnily enough, when I was at Glentoran, I had a friend who was in the weight-training business – he was Mr Ireland actually – a fellow called Buster McShane [later the coach of Olympic gold medallist Mary Peters] ... a great pal of mine; we went to school together ... and Buster said to me, 'You should come into our gym and train with weights.' So, unbeknown to the Glentoran management, I went in and trained with power weights ... to build up some upper body strength ... I always had good legs but I had a light body.

By the end of the 1950–51 season, Bingham had passed two significant landmarks: becoming an established first-team player at Roker Park; and winning his first cap for Northern Ireland, against France in Belfast on 12 May 1951. His display on the latter occasion earned the respect of the opposition left-back Roger Marche who, years later and after winning nearly fifty caps for France, would name Bingham as the most difficult opponent he ever faced.

Bingham played a total of eight seasons for Sunderland, making 206 league appearances and scoring forty-five goals, but the club itself never quite fulfilled its potential. Despite an impressive array of talent, including Bingham and the legendary inside-forward Len Shackleton, and a willingness to spend lavishly on strengthening the team (earning the unofficial title of the 'Bank of England' club), the closest Sunderland came to success was in 1954–55 when they finished fourth in the First Division and reached the semi-finals of the FA Cup.

After the World Cup in Sweden, Bingham moved on to Luton Town, then Everton and finally Port Vale, all the time turning in consistent displays for Northern Ireland and eventually equalling Danny Blanchflower's total of fifty-six caps. Arguably the World Cup adventure found him at his peak.

Playing alongside Bingham for Northern Ireland, as he had for Glentoran and the international youth team, was perhaps the greatest British inside-forward of his era. That was certainly the opinion of one of England's greatest ever players, Stanley Matthews, who said of Jimmy McIlroy: 'When he is at his best, he takes command of the game ... Subtlety dominates his game, and this allied to the ability to read a match, and find the open space in a flash, makes him a foe to be feared by all opponents.'[2] Praise indeed.

Jimmy McIlroy was born in Lambeg, between Belfast and Lisburn, on 25 October 1931. He was the only boy in a family of five and therefore the only one with a prospect of carrying on the family's proud footballing tradition. His father, Harry, played for Distillery, but rarely in the first team, while his uncle Willie McIlroy played centre-half for Portadown and regularly gave his nephew a football as a Christmas present. Jimmy soon showed signs that he might well be the most outstanding McIlroy footballer of them all, competing with and often dominating much older boys in matches at Lambeg Public Elementary School.

Harry McIlroy recognised that his son might have a bright future ahead of him as a footballer and went to great lengths to assist his prospects, even insisting that when rationing continued in the post-war period, Jimmy should be the best fed of all the family. The views of Jimmy's sisters are not recorded. It was also with the aim of developing McIlroy's physique, to complement his innate skill, that a cousin suggested he start work as a bricklayer, this in 1947. One of the brickies the sixteen-year-old found himself working alongside was his future Northern Ireland colleague Tommy Casey, but in truth both found the job harrowing, especially in winter.

It was Glentoran FC that came to Jimmy's rescue, having watched him playing for the Craigavad club near Bangor and being duly impressed. McIlroy recounted how he was approached by the Glentoran scout Fred Steadman:

> One Sunday night, strolling through Lisburn with another boy from Lambeg village, Arthur Taylor, I was stopped by Mr Steadman. He asked Arthur and I if we would like to become Glentoran players. He had no need to ask twice. We promptly put our names to the forms, and received our signing-on fee ... a fish-and-chip supper![3]

Shades of Ashley Cole and Chelsea ... or perhaps not.

Glentoran was the perfect club for a classy player like McIlroy – a real football academy. His manager in the Glens junior team, former international John Geary, encouraged what might be called cultured football – the emphasis was on passing and movement rather than force – which was exactly what Jimmy McIlroy was cut out for. It was here too that he met up for the first time with another future Northern Ireland colleague, Billy Bingham.

McIlroy made his breakthrough into the Glentoran first team in the last month of the 1948–49 season and, with Bingham, became a regular in the side in 1949–50. Amazingly it was only now that he decided to give up bricklaying, no longer able to cope with two jobs, but as a result having to rely henceforth on a modest weekly wage of £5 from the Glens. However, he did not have to rely on that fiver for very long.

McIlroy was clearly a player of potential though of limited experience at senior level. Nonetheless, Burnley had been watching him for some time and by March 1950 had clearly seen enough to convince them that £8,000 – the price it would take for Glentoran to release McIlroy – was an investment worth making, even if he was only eighteen years old without even one full season under his belt. To say that he was worth every penny would be similar to describing George Best as a tricky winger.

At first, McIlroy wondered what he had let himself in for. Booked into a hotel in Burnley, he remembers the scene that greeted him from the window that first morning. It had been market day the day before, and bits of hay and old packaging and general litter were swirling about in an early breeze. It did not look terribly inviting. On top of that there was the unwanted early morning alarm call from hundreds of clogged feet as the early shift made their way to the local factories. Was this an English town or the 'Village of the Damned'?

But it got better. Jimmy McIlroy and Burnley were meant for each other – their common hallmark was football played with style and composure. His record with the north-west club speaks for itself: 439 league games (1950–51 to 1962–63), 116 league goals and a League Championship medal. It was during his second season with Burnley that McIlroy made the first of his fifty-five appearances for Northern Ireland (against Scotland in October 1951), a total that included all the qualifying and final tournament games in the 1958 World Cup. Burnley regarded McIlroy as their greatest asset in this period; he was arguably also the jewel in the crown for Northern Ireland.

Unfortunately his playing career with Burnley ended prematurely when chairman Bob Lord, according to McIlroy, took a dislike to him because of his friendship with the club's vice-chairman. When Danny Blanchflower heard that McIlroy was on the transfer list, he immediately phoned his Northern Ireland colleague to find out why, as he wanted to write a piece for the Sunday papers about it. When McIlroy explained, Blanchflower's sceptical response was to inquire if Jimmy had been messing about with Lord's daughters, to which McIlroy answered, 'Have you seen them?' Enough said.

Still, even when he left the club to join Stoke City, he continued to live in Burnley – and still does. 'Some people ask me if I never think of moving home,' he smiles. 'But where's home? I've lived here since I was eighteen, fifty-eight years ago.' He says this, mind you, in an unmistakable Ulster accent.

If Northern Ireland had been able to pick a player of the calibre of Jimmy McIlroy in the other inside-forward position, or at centre-forward, they might have done even better in Sweden in 1958, but those positions remained a problem for the men in green. Throughout the period in question McIlroy had no regular partner at inside-forward, the place variously filled by Jackie Blanchflower, Wilbur Cush, Tommy Casey and others. At centre-forward no one player was dominant, Doherty at different times calling on the services of Eddie McMorran, Jimmy Jones, Billy McAdams and Billy Simpson. In fact in the five games that Northern Ireland played in the 1958 World Cup finals, no fewer than four players filled the centre-forward position.

Eddie McMorran, who was born in Larne on 2 September 1923, played junior football for Ballyclare Paper Mill and his home town club before joining Belfast Celtic. From there he moved to Manchester City where in two seasons he made thirty-three league appearances and scored twelve league goals. After leaving Maine Road he played for a couple of seasons at Leeds and then spent the rest of his career in the lower reaches of the League, with Barnsley, Doncaster Rovers and Crewe Alexandra.

Billy McAdams was another who made the breakthrough into English football with Manchester City. A native of Belfast, born on 20 January 1934, he had played Irish League football with Distillery before City made an offer for him in December 1953. In seven seasons at Maine Road, McAdams scored sixty-two league goals in 127 games, a not unimpressive total but not one he was able to match at international level.

Similarly Jimmy Jones was a prolific scorer in the Irish League with Belfast Celtic and Glenavon. His local career spanned twenty years and almost 750 goals but the gulf between local and international football was not one that could easily be bridged. Jones in fact won only three caps for Northern Ireland.

Probably the pick of the crop of Northern Ireland centre-forwards of this era was Billy Simpson. He played in local football for Linfield, with whom he enjoyed considerable success, helping them win the Irish League in 1948–49 (topping the scoring charts with nineteen goals) and 1949–50 and the Irish Cup in 1948 and 1950 (scoring in the 1948 final against Coleraine). Inevitably Simpson's prowess as a goalscorer soon attracted the attention of the British professional game and he was sold to Scottish giants Rangers for a then record fee for the Glasgow club of £11,500. He proved to be well worth the money, scoring 163 goals in all competitions and helping Rangers win three Scottish championships and the Scottish Cup once. After leaving Ibrox he remained in Scottish football with Stirling Albion. For Northern Ireland, Simpson's record was a very creditable five goals in twelve games but injury was to rob him and the international side of the opportunity to make his mark in Sweden.

Ironically it was at the final stages of the 1958 World Cup that Northern Ireland unearthed a centre-forward talent who had promise but at this stage, still quite a few rough edges. Derek Dougan had grown up in east Belfast in a football-loving home – his father supported Glentoran while his grandfather had played centre-half for Linfield. The young Dougan was also a centre-half in his early career, which encompassed Greggagh Boys Club (where George Best would later emerge), Linfield and Distillery, with whom he won the Irish Cup. Like Billy Bingham, Dougan also served an apprenticeship at Harland and Wolff, but a switch to centre-forward at the start of the 1957–58 season proved to be a turning point in his life. He was signed by Portsmouth and made his debut in an impressive 3-0 victory against Manchester United at Old Trafford. Dougan's leap up the football ladder caught the attention of the Northern Ireland selectors, and Peter Doherty, and the nineteen-year-old found himself bound for Sweden. For Derek Dougan, of course, the best days were yet to come.

If Northern Ireland lacked an imposing presence at centre-forward, there were no such shortcomings at outside-left. Peter McParland was not an orthodox left-winger in the style of say Davie Cooper at Rangers, Eddie Gray at Leeds or Peter Barnes and Ryan Giggs at Manchester City and United respectively. McParland had a more direct style, liking to attack from the wing but zeroing in very quickly on the opposing goal. He was a hard-as-iron player who was an intimidating presence in any forward line. He certainly left his mark on the 1957 FA Cup final, thundering into the Manchester United goalkeeper Ray Wood, who had to retire injured as a result, and scoring both of his team's goals to help Aston Villa lift the Cup for the seventh time.

McParland was born in Newry on 25 April 1934, like Jimmy McIlroy the only boy in a family of five. His home was in Chapel Street and his local school was the Christian Brothers. Here the young McParland was able to play only

Gaelic football (the 'association' variety was banned) but this undoubtedly helped him become the player he did: strong, energetic, fearless. With McParland as captain, the school team won the Macrory Cup two years in succession.

McParland, however, wanted to play football, and to such an extent that he set up his own team. When he left school at age fourteen he helped found the Shamrock Youth Club which competed in and enjoyed considerable success in the Newry and District Summer League. The man brought in to manage the outfit was Frank O'Hanlon and it was he who took care to groom the young McParland for future stardom.

After a friendly game against Dundalk, McParland was offered a contract by the County Louth side, meanwhile working variously as an apprentice barman and then in a timber yard. The move to Dundalk did, however, bring him to the attention of the professional game in England and at the age of just sixteen he was offered a trial by Leeds United. Unfortunately by the time McParland made it to Elland Road, he was still recovering from sea-sickness and was unable to do himself justice.

So, it was back to Dundalk and his senior debut against Bohemians in September 1950, scoring twice in a 5-2 victory. At the same time he also started a new job at the Great Northern Railway yard in the town. McParland was still attracting notice from across the Irish Sea and in 1951 Leicester City made an offer to take him to Filbert Street. Possibly mindful of what had happened at Leeds, and advised by his father to wait a little longer and gain more experience before going to England, McParland refused the offer and bided his time. It was not a decision he was to regret.

At the start of the 1952–53 season, a number of clubs showed interest in signing McParland, and he chose Aston Villa in preference to Southampton, Hull City and Birmingham City. It was again a decision influenced by his father who had worked in Birmingham during the war and sent home regular reports of his visits to Villa Park. Villa also had Danny Blanchflower on the books, though McParland, despite the £3,800 transfer fee, would not have been expecting to line up alongside Danny in the first team just yet.

In fact, he would have to wait seventeen months before his debut in the senior side, but that game was important for another reason. In the reserves McParland had been playing regularly at left-half, and before that had always played at inside-left, but the opportunity to play in the first team was at outside-left. The opponents were Wolverhampton Wanderers on Christmas Eve 1953; McParland scored the winning goal. He retained his place and never looked back (or inside).

Three months later, McParland made his first appearance for Northern Ireland, against Wales at Wrexham on 31 March 1954. Maintaining his record of debut goals, the left-winger netted twice to give Northern Ireland a 2-1 win, their first victory under Peter Doherty. His first goal in fact came after only forty seconds, lobbing the ball past the helpless Jack Kelsey who was winning his first cap for Wales. It was in the Wrexham match that a new Northern Ireland clearly began to take shape. This was their last game in that season's British Home Championship, which also served as a qualifying group for the World Cup, and having already lost to England and Scotland, Doherty decided to introduce a number of new players.

Apart from McParland, debuts were also given to Harry Gregg, Bertie Peacock and Jackie Blanchflower. Although it had a new look to it the team did benefit from the fact that a number of players had been together in the international youth side, so the likes of Bingham, McIlroy and Jackie Blanchflower had a level of cohesion which they now brought to the full international team. It was still a young side however – average age twenty-three – but Doherty would carefully nurture it to maturity over the next few years. The 2-1 victory was then something of an omen for the future.

As for McParland he was to become something of a Villa legend. Apart from scoring the goals that won the 1957 FA Cup final, in nine seasons at Villa Park, he played 293 league games and was just two short of a century of league goals. Billy Wright, captain of England for most of the 1950s, when asked to pick a representative team for that era, said that Peter McParland would be one of his first choices. Jimmy McIlroy likens him to Ronaldo of Manchester United in the modern game; high praise indeed. McParland played out his career with Wolves and Plymouth, and won thirty-four caps for Northern Ireland; one of the all-time greats without a doubt.

An important, though non-playing, member of the Northern Ireland set-up was the trainer Gerry Morgan. A former player with Linfield and now the club's trainer, Morgan cut an incongruous figure considering his title. Bald, possessing only two front teeth, and evidently not personally devoted to staying in shape, Morgan looked a comic character and acted as unofficial jester to the team.

He was the heart and soul of the side off the pitch, famous for such sayings as that Northern Ireland's principal tactic was to equalise before the opposition scored, often asking players, 'Did you clean your teeth today – both of them?' which was all the funnier coming from someone so dentally challenged. Gerry's banter and upbeat outlook on life ensured that the mood in the Northern Ireland dressing room was always positive.

Jimmy McIlroy comments: 'I honestly don't know how much he knew about injuries or how to treat them, but he certainly made up for it in maintaining team spirit in the side.' He was 'a laugh a minute' according to Peter McParland, though not everyone appreciated his routine at the World Cup of doing the rounds at 7.30 in the morning with a glass of health salts for each player.

One of Gerry's party pieces, as Harry Gregg remembers, was a mock commentary on the Grand National. Apparently this was a particular favourite of the FA Secretary Sir Stanley Rous who would often call on Morgan to perform it at the post-match banquet when England played Northern Ireland. Gerry certainly enjoyed England–Northern Ireland encounters and would give a running commentary as the team bus travelled from the hotel to Wembley or wherever, making remarks such as 'We are now passing a large pub ... Why?'

Gregg also remembers Morgan's antics when the international squad visited the cinema to see a gangster film the night before the England–Northern Ireland game at Wembley in November 1957. Gerry kept the players amused – egged on by Jackie Blanchflower but most certainly not by brother Danny – by shouting out 'Watch out!' or 'He's in the cupboard!' at appropriate junctures in relation to the on-screen action. The usherette was at her wits' end trying to find out who was causing the commotion and eventually the film had to be stopped and the lights put on for pandemonium was about to break out in the upper circle. As Gregg concluded, 'There were no low spirits when he [Morgan] was [around].'

Jimmy McIlroy recalls one occasion when Peter McParland had taken a knock in a match and had been treated by Gerry and then advised by the trainer to move out to the wing for a while to recover (as was the usual practice in a time before substitutes). It was only as he moved to the position that the thought struck McParland, 'Wait a minute, I play on the wing – I'm a winger,' but that was Morgan, always able to raise a smile, no matter what the circumstances.

Another Morgan–McParland episode is also worth relaying. A Northern Ireland–Scotland match was due to be televised – a novelty in that pre-Sky era – and Gerry wanted to get 'on the box'. Peter McParland, therefore, volunteered to feign injury towards the end of the game to give Gerry his moment of fame, if a genuine injury had not already by that stage brought the trainer onto the field of play.

In the event, eighty-seven minutes of the game had elapsed without Gerry's services being called upon, so with three minutes left, Peter McParland duly fell to the ground. The only problem was that this wasn't an act – he was suffering from severe leg cramp. Gerry trotted on in glorious monochrome, beaming smiles, and, winking and grinning, bent over the prostrate McParland. The referee came over and asked the Northern Ireland trainer what was the matter with the player. Still smiling down at McParland, Gerry responded: 'I think it must be old age.'[4]

With the unprecedented talent that Northern Ireland football had at its disposal in the late 1950s, would it have mattered who the manager was? In other words, could Peter Doherty simply have sat back, as was supposedly Matt Busby's style, and told the players to do the business? Billy Bingham, who was to manage a very successful Northern Ireland side in the 1980s, responds to that question with an emphatic 'no', and elaborates, 'He wasn't in that position. I think that he had the nucleus of a good side ... but there was always "fill-ins"' – who remain unidentified. On the other hand, there were, as Bingham puts it, 'the ones who were there constantly with Peter ... He trusted us and we produced.'

By January 1957, Northern Ireland, for the first time in its history, had a manager, captain and team ready to take on the best in international football. But not even the most optimistic observer could have anticipated the events that were to unfold in the next eighteen months.

1. Jimmy McIlroy, *Right Inside Soccer*, The Sportsman's Book Club, 1961, p. 109.
2. McIlroy, foreword.
3. Ibid., p. 14.
4. Peter McParland, *Going for Goal*, Souvenir Press Ltd, 1960, p. 25.

THREE

In Pursuit of the 'Glittering Prize'

Although Northern Ireland was the smallest of the fifty-three nations to set out on the quest for qualification for the finals of the 1958 World Cup, they were not intimidated by the prospect of competing with foreign opposition to achieve that goal. This was not a reflection on the merit of that opposition, for the history of the World Cup to that point was proof of the ability of the continental and South American teams, but rather on the insularity of the British game. Martin Lee, of the *Sporting Chronicle*, had made the pertinent observation in 1951: 'Soccer on the Continent, to many Britishers, is rather like a minor revolution in a far-off land. You hear about the result, and the effect it has on the local inhabitants, but it is seldom capable of provoking a personal reaction.'[1]

Admittedly, Lee's comment was penned before Hungary shook English football to the core with those remarkable victories at Wembley in 1953 and in Budapest (7-1) the following year, but once the shock waves had settled, the old self-assurance soon reasserted itself. The prevalent attitude in football in the off-shore isles remained 'British is best', though because Northern Ireland had always been the junior partners in terms of UK football there was no false optimism going into the tournament. In the much scaled-down competition that the World Cup was in the 1950s, compared to today's extravaganza, Northern Ireland were placed in a group of just three teams with only one qualifying for the finals. Their opponents were Italy, the only team to have won the World Cup in consecutive competitions (1934 and 1938), and Portugal, whom they would meet in the opening match. Although the Portuguese did not have a World Cup track record to match Italy's, their recent form indicated that they would be no pushovers. They had defeated Spain 3-1, drawn 2-2 with Hungary, and lost only 1-0 to Brazil, all the games played in Lisbon. As Jimmy McIlroy reflects:

> To be honest I didn't think we had a ghost of a chance of making progress but it was exciting for all of us, the very fact that we were playing in the World Cup and playing against teams of this calibre. I don't think any of us would have placed a bet that Ireland would qualify for the finals.

Lisbon now beckoned Northern Ireland for the opening encounter on 16 January 1957. The team assembled the previous weekend at the Kenilworth Hotel in London, only twelve players making the trip, a sign not only that this was the pre-substitute era but also that Northern Ireland was a region of limited resources, at least in terms of quantity. But what they may have lacked in numbers they more than compensated for in spirit. Before leaving London, manager Doherty called them to their purpose: 'We go out to fight for the honour of Northern Ireland and for the glittering prize of a place in the World Cup final sixteen. Remember, we are ambassadors for our country.'[2]

Travelling to Portugal fifty years ago was a much more exciting, and, in some respects, arduous prospect than it is today. The BEA Viscount flight that the Northern Ireland party boarded on Monday, 14 January took four hours to reach its destination, but nothing could detract from the lure of the exotic in this pre-package travel age. Malcolm Brodie captured the closing stages of the journey in the style of an adventure story, which of course it was:

> Emerging from a quilt of white, fleeced clouds, below us lay the Tagus and a panorama of colour. On the right, anchored, moored or in motion were many types of ships, barges laden with cork, small naval craft, freighters, sardine and shrimp boats.
> To the North lay Lisbon, to the South the ferry terminus of Cacilhas.[3]

The Northern Ireland team was based at the Palace Hotel, while the game itself was to be played at the home of Sporting Lisbon, the 60,000-capacity Alvalade Stadium, or in Portuguese the Estadio Jose de Alvalade. This was also to be the first floodlit international in Portugal, kick-off scheduled for the unusually late time of 9.45pm. Late, that is, if you're not Portuguese. Some readers may remember twenty-four years later when Northern Ireland had fought a gallant 0-0 home draw with Scotland which looked like it meant failure to qualify for Spain '82, only for the joyous news to reach Ulster that Northern Ireland's rivals for a place in the World Cup finals, Portugal, had lost at home to Sweden in a game that had only started when most Northern Ireland fans were thinking of going to bed. Yes, the Portuguese do like their night-time football, but it doesn't always like them. Peter Doherty, in fact, thought that the late start might be to his team's advantage in terms of the temperature, the Ulstermen being no strangers to the cold.

They might, however, have been surprised by the national anthem which the Portuguese Football Federation originally proposed to play in honour of their visitors. Apparently the hosts were not quite certain about Northern Ireland's constitutional position (but then who is?) and had initially contacted the Republic of Ireland's minister in Lisbon,

Thomas Vincent Cummins, to request the words and music of the Irish national anthem. It was only then that they discovered that the 'Northern' in Northern Ireland did have a special significance. The faux pas was averted and 'God Save the Queen' swiftly substituted for 'The Soldier's Song' in the pre-match schedule, but the Portuguese authorities now veered to the opposite extreme and on the match programme cover had printed the Union Jack, rather than the Ulster flag, alongside the national flag of Portugal.

It was cold all day on Wednesday, 16 January, cold enough to keep the crowd well below capacity (around 30,000 were present) while many of those who attended wrapped themselves in blankets against the elements. However, the atmosphere was passionate and was further stimulated by a lap of honour by the Portuguese Olympic side before the kick-off and apparently there was some sort of reception for the winner of the Boston marathon as Peter McParland recalls. Stimulating is not exactly how McParland would describe the delay his team had to endure:

> We got the message to go down to the tunnel ... a fair old walk [in the stadium to get to the top of the tunnel]. When we got down there we were told, 'You can't go out yet.' There was a celebration for this fellow [who had won the marathon], they were going to give him a sort of reception. And we were waiting in there for about half an hour and we didn't go back [to the changing room] ... we stood around there. Peter was livid ... The Portuguese played a trick on us there, [they] tried one on ... They upset us ... it backfired on them.

It was after 10 o'clock before the game was ready to start but Doherty believed his side was well prepared for the challenge to come. After the tunnel escapade, no one needed geeing up for this encounter. (Wilbur Cush had already received the boost of a good-luck letter from five girls at his work in Lurgan, the letter carrying not just their signatures but their lipstick kisses as well!) The respective line-ups were as follows:

Portugal: Gomes (Sporting Lisbon); Virgilio (FC Porto), Angelo (Benfica); Pedroto (FC Porto), Pussos (Sporting Lisbon), Costa (FC Porto); Hernani (FC Porto), Vasques (Sporting Lisbon), Aguas (Benfica), Coluna (Benfica), Perdiago (FC Porto).

Northern Ireland: Gregg (Doncaster Rovers); Cunningham (Leicester City), McMichael (Newcastle United); Blanchflower, D (Tottenham Hotspur), Blanchflower, J (Manchester United), Casey (Newcastle United); Bingham (Sunderland), McIlroy (Burnley), Coyle (Coleraine), Cush (Glenavon), McParland (Aston Villa).

Danny Blanchflower would again be Doherty's commander on the field, with the authority to change tactics if in his opinion it was necessary. That looked very unlikely as Northern Ireland hit the ground running, taking the game to their opponents. After just five minutes the visitors won a corner which Peter McParland swung over. An attempted flick-on by McIlroy did not come off but the ball fell to Bingham who struck it cleanly with his weaker left foot into the Portuguese net.

'I think I whacked it,' Bingham says with a smile on his face, 'and it was from a distance – well, twenty-odd yards – and it went sailing right into the corner. It was one of those ones that you dream of.' The goal was celebrated on the pitch but was greeted by a deathly silence off it.

The goal was a sign of things to come. Bingham, in particular, was in inspired form and was unlucky not to score again when, after beating left-back Angelo, he sent in a cross-cum-shot which ran across the face of the Portuguese crossbar. A McParland effort from the left suffered a similar fate but it was not all one-way traffic. Portugal also hit the bar with a shot from inside-left Coluna but on the whole the Northern Ireland defence looked comfortable, Jackie Blanchflower marking Portugal's star centre-forward Jose Aguas out of the game. In the middle of the field, Cush and Casey were tackling tenaciously, allowing Northern Ireland to remain in the ascendant.

Then disaster. With a little over ten minutes of the first half remaining, Portugal won a corner on the left. When the ball came over it was headed home easily by inside-right Vasques with Gregg apparently rooted to the spot. After such a sterling performance it was a wrenching blow and Tommy Casey, who had been excelling at wing-half, could not contain his frustration with Gregg. Jimmy McIlroy witnessed the exchange:

> [Casey shouted] 'What's the matter with you?' Said Gregg, 'The lights dazzled me.' That excuse didn't satisfy Tommy who cracked, 'There are twenty-one other players here who manage to see the ball.' Harry Gregg exploded: 'Come you in if you think you can do any better.'[4]

Casey did not take up the invitation, nor did Bertie Peacock, sitting on the bench, accept Peter Doherty's proposal that he run over to Gregg to try to calm him down. Putting self-preservation above all else, Bertie declined to go anywhere near the 'keeper who had already exploded once and might well do so again. It was a disheartened Northern Ireland that left the field at half-time with the score at 1-1.

If the initiative was now with the home side, it was the briefest of possessions. Doherty's team, in the image of their master, were not content with a draw and continued to mount attack after attack in the second half. Only heroics by Gomes in the Portuguese goal, making point-blank saves from Cush and McIlroy, kept the scores level. If there was a likely winner here, it was not going to be Gomes' team.

Frustrated by their failure to impose themselves on supposedly weaker opposition, Portugal increasingly resorted to roughhouse tactics to put Northern Ireland off their game. The French referee Marcel Lequesne turned a blind eye to the Iberians' indiscretions on a number of occasions – an obvious 'homer' in today's parlance – letting the game turn uglier by the minute. When Northern Ireland centre-forward Coyle collided with Gomes, the Ulsterman found himself lying on the ground where he was blatantly kicked by the Portuguese left-back Angelo. M. Lequesne's response was to award a free-kick to the home side for the challenge on the 'keeper, and give the bemused Coyle a ticking off.

Northern Ireland had their moments too in terms of exercising their physical presence and during the course of the second half, three Portuguese players had to leave the field for treatment. Indeed the correspondent of the *Irish News* was of the opinion that 'Irish roughness made the Portuguese lose their calm'.[5]

Trying to apportion blame between the two sides does not, however, exonerate the referee for failing to exert his authority and restore order. It was interesting too that the after-match comments of Benfica's Brazilian trainer Otto Gloria stressed the positive in Northern Ireland's performance: 'The Irish were individually perfect and in spite of their team being composed from many clubs they showed a remarkable cohesion.'[6]

The chief victim of the Portuguese assaults was Peter McParland. His forays down the wing left the Portuguese right-back Virgilio floundering – he could not counteract McParland by fair means and had no hesitation in turning to foul. What may have been the choicest of a real *cordon bleu* selection of illegal challenges was his grabbing McParland's shirt after the latter had again got round him, holding on until it began to rip off the Newry man's back and, as the *pièce de résistance*, finally bringing his man down with a rugby tackle. *Olé!* as the Spanish say, or indeed *Voilà!* from M. Lequesne.

Later the Northern Ireland left-winger narrowly avoided a lunging knee-high tackle from the Portuguese right-back, but this time Virgilio failed in his mission to destroy. However, as often as not, if McParland managed to evade Virgilio there was someone to take his place. Just such an incident ensued in the sixty-first minute.

McParland had broken through the Portuguese rearguard and a winner looked in prospect, when left-half Costa, who had slipped to the ground, decided he wanted some company and grabbed the Northern Ireland left-winger's ankles to take him off his feet. Today it would mean a red card and dismissal; it should have produced the same result on that occasion. What did actually happen? Nothing. *Formidable!* (Marcel Lequesne was apparently no stranger to controversy and his name was again in the spotlight when he officiated in the second leg of the European Cup semi-final between Manchester United and Real Madrid at Old Trafford in April. With the scores level at 2-2, the crowd had been anticipating about three or four minutes of injury time in view of the number of stoppages in the second half but the French referee seemed to make no allowance for this, blowing the final whistle on ninety minutes, thereby denying United the possibility of a late winner.)

The final score in Lisbon was 1-1 but it was something of a moral victory for Northern Ireland that all eleven players were able to walk off the pitch at the end. They would need a few new shirts, though.

Northern Ireland had a little over three months to wait until their next group match, but it was a much anticipated encounter: against the world champions of 1934 and 1938, Italy, in Rome. In the interim, the team had one outing, a scoreless draw against Wales at Windsor Park in the British Championship on 10 April. If this suggests that the players were well rested for the Rome match, nothing could be further from the truth. The game was scheduled for Thursday, 25 April but over the previous weekend – Easter of 1957 – most of the Northern Ireland team had played three matches for their club sides (Friday, Saturday and Monday). Little wonder that the Italian press were astounded by such a build-up to a World Cup qualifier, especially when contrasted with the preparations of their own national team who had two weeks to themselves at their secluded training camp. To cap this, the Italians were also on a win bonus of £100-a-man, a lot of money in the mid-1950s.

A further handicap for Northern Ireland was the upcoming FA Cup final between Aston Villa and Manchester United. In an era when club always took priority over country, Villa's Peter McParland and United's Jackie Blanchflower, two of Northern Ireland's best players against Portugal, would not be available for selection because of the Wembley fixture. For a team with Northern Ireland's limited resources this meant some serious reshuffling; Blanchflower's place was to be filled by Wilbur Cush, who had played at inside-left against Portugal (but was normally a wing-half!); while Bertie Peacock, normally a left-half, was drafted in to take McParland's place at outside-left.

McParland is adamant that he wanted to play but was browbeaten by his club:

> The Villa played a trick on me [a favourite expression of McParland's] and I was annoyed with them over that ... I said I wanted to play for Ireland in Italy, and they said what about if you get injured and I said this is the chance [to play in the World Cup] and I want to take it ... but

they put a ban on me and wouldn't release me ... It was
the chairman of the Villa who pushed that [ban] and I
was annoyed over that.

No such complications bedevilled the Italians, who
fielded a side based on the rock-solid defence of Fiorentina,
champions of Italy and European Cup finalists against Real
Madrid. Northern Ireland's selection problems must have
been a further boon to the Italy team, but what exactly they
made of the choice of the vertically challenged Cush to play
at centre-half is open to speculation; the Italian press were
certainly bemused.

Cush, nonetheless, was having a great season for Glenavon, captaining the Lurgan side to an Irish League and Cup
double and being named Ulster Footballer of the Year by
local football writers, commentators and referees. He had
also played at centre-half for Northern Ireland in that game
against Wales in Belfast on 10 April and had kept the Welsh
centre-forward John Charles at bay. Jimmy McIlroy has vivid
memories of that encounter:

We were playing Wales ... and centre-forward that day
for Wales was John Charles. Centre-half for Ireland was
5ft 6ins Wilbur Cush. It could only happen in an Irish side
... I think when people saw them lining up they thought,
'There's a catch in this'. And yet I can remember a year
or two after this there was some function in Belfast ...
and we were all in this lounge, and John Charles came
through the door and he looked across the room and he
pointed a finger at Wilbur, 'You see that little ____ ... I
played against him ... and I never won a ball in the air.'
And John Charles to me at that time was the best centre-
forward, the best centre-half in the world, 6ft 2ins or
something, and magnificent in the air. That night it just
seemed as if Wilbur climbed up his back ...

Cush was then as ready as any of his team-mates for the challenge ahead. On the day the teams lined up as follows:

Italy: Lovati (Lazio); Magnini (Fiorentina), Cervato (Fiorentina); Chiapella (Fiorentina), Orzan (Fiorentina), Segato (Fiorentina); Muncinelli (Lazio), Gali (AC Milan), Firmani (Sampdoria), Gratton (Fiorentina), Frignani (AC Udinese).

Northern Ireland: Gregg (Doncaster Rovers); Cunningham (Leicester City), McMichael (Newcastle United); Blanchflower (Tottenham Hotspur), Cush (Glenavon), Casey (Newcastle United); Bingham (Sunderland), McIlroy (Burnley), Simpson (Rangers), McMorran (Doncaster Rovers), Peacock (Celtic).

The Northern Ireland squad – if that is not too grand a title for the total of thirteen players who were taken to Rome (the eleven above plus Jackie Scott of Grimsby Town and Dick Keith of Newcastle United) – arrived in the Italian capital on the Tuesday, 23 April after a five-hour flight from Luton airport. There was great interest in the game, and not just locally, for it was to be shown to an estimated TV audience of ten million in Britain, France, Holland, Switzerland, Germany and Austria. The match was scheduled for Liberation Day, a public holiday, and there was a thriving black market for tickets with those carrying a face value of between 9s and £5 being sold for anything from 25s to £20. There was a real football buzz in the air, especially as the news had just broken that the Welsh international John Charles had been transferred from Leeds to Juventus.

In Portugal, Northern Ireland had played in the cold of a mid-winter night, but in the 100,000-capacity Olympic Stadium in Rome, Peter Doherty's team faced a much less hospitable 75-degree heat. In the preliminaries to the game itself, each Northern Ireland player received a bunch of flowers (something we are more accustomed to at great sporting occasions today), and they created a good impression with the Italian supporters by throwing the bouquets into the crowd. With the niceties completed, battle was ready to commence.

As it transpired, the decisive moment of the match came as early as the third minute. Italy were awarded a free-kick about twenty-five yards from goal, in response to which Northern Ireland set up a defensive wall. This was a tactic that was still very much in its infancy in 1957 and subject therefore to imperfections and misapplication. At first, centre-half Orzan lined up to take the kick but he was pushed aside by left-back Sergio Cervato. At that moment the referee was getting the Northern Ireland wall to move back the statutory ten yards, allowing Cervato to move the ball to the right and take the kick while the visitors' defence was still disorganised. Harry Gregg was as unprepared as his team-mates for the shot, and the ball sailed past him into the net. Gamesmanship had played a large part in the goal, but it was a goal nonetheless.

Even before the game, Northern Ireland had been portrayed as lambs to the slaughter; now, a goal down with only three minutes gone, the slaughter was expected to commence in earnest. It didn't. The defence may have been outmanoeuvred for the goal, but they quickly regained their composure and kept the Italians at bay. At left-back, Alfie McMichael gave probably his best performance to date in the international team while the stop-gap centre-half Wilbur Cush played the Italian centre-forward, Eddie Firmani, out of the game. Firmani, then of Sampdoria but no stranger to the British game as a former player with Charlton Athletic, duly acknowledged Cush's sterling qualities: 'He was like a brick wall. I couldn't go through him.'[7]

In goal, Harry Gregg, far from allowing the goal to unnerve him, went on to give an outstanding display, inspiring his colleagues which correspondingly had a dispiriting effect on the opposition. The only occasion when he may have been considered fortuitous was when an effort from Firmani struck him in the face, but that aside, this was an assured exposition. The highlight was probably an acrobatic palm over the bar from Muncinelli's shot in the closing minutes of the first half, when the Italians were pushing hard for a second goal. Gregg had to be at his best because the Italian midfield was inventive and creative, setting up chance after chance for their forwards, but most of these moves foundered on the rock that was the Doncaster Rovers and Northern Ireland 'keeper.

Indeed, such was the quality of Gregg's performance that his name was subsequently linked with a possible move to Genoa. It was a rumour quickly scotched by Peter Doherty, who was also the 'keeper's club manager at Doncaster Rovers; on the flight home, Doherty assured the travelling press that Harry Gregg would not be going anywhere until he considered the time and the team was right. Whatever the outcome for Gregg's career, he certainly had made an impression on the Italian footballing public, evidenced by the approach of a sports shop owner when the Northern Ireland 'keeper was shopping in the city before the flight home. Presenting Gregg with a pair of boots, he said, 'For you, Mr Gregg, take them.'[8] It surely cannot have happened to many visiting goalkeepers.

In the middle of the field, Danny Blanchflower played a captain's part, putting behind him the lacklustre showing in Lisbon. Malcolm Brodie eulogised in his match report: 'Here was the complete craftsman, brilliant on the ball in defence and attack, covering up struggling colleagues and spurring on his shot shy forwards.'[9]

Brodie's observations highlighted Northern Ireland's main shortcoming in the game, a not unfamiliar one, though the problem was not so much that the attackers were shot shy as goal shy. Blanchflower hit the bar after a corner-kick and Simpson and McIlroy were also denied by the woodwork, this action all packed into a frenetic last ten minutes when the visitors put the Italians on the back foot in the ultimately vain quest for an equaliser. McIlroy admitted that his shot from just twelve yards should really have found the net – 'I have nightmares even yet … Oh, if that only had gone in … it would have made things a bit easier for us' – but even in defeat he took comfort from the way the team had played:

> Coming off the field, I realized for the first time that Northern Ireland were good enough to qualify for the World Cup. We had invaded enemy territory twice to discover we were every bit as good as Portugal and Italy. We had seen the best they had to offer and I couldn't wait to get them back to Windsor Park, Belfast for the home matches.[10]

Danny Blanchflower, speaking more in the style of a co-manager than captain, was also encouraged that Northern Ireland had held their own:

> I don't think we deserved to lose. A draw would have been better, but I am very satisfied by our play. We are unused to the light ball and hard pitches. The ground was good and though we suffered from the heat, I was very surprised to see it affected the Italians worse. We had more energy in the end and lasted better.[11]

Those were sentiments shared by the off-the-field contingent as well. IFA Secretary Billy Drennan organised an impromptu 'celebration' in the dressing room, where the iced tea flowed like Italian wine (along with some Italian wine). Drennan remarked afterwards:

> I know it seems daft celebrating a defeat … But we were

fully expecting to be given a good rousing. Instead it nearly ended up the other way round.

The Italians just didn't have the finish we expected. On the defence they were superb at the beginning, but they never seemed to get moving together in attack, despite their wonderful ground passing. They had plenty of chances, but never made the most of them.[12]

Team manager Doherty, too, was in a positive frame of mind after the game, particularly considering the advantage the home side had had in terms of preparing for this contest:

We'll have their measure next time we meet … All our boys played a normal league match on Monday with their own teams. The Italians should have been much better than they were …[13]

The reaction of the home supporters to the 1-0 win gave credence to Doherty's verdict. They threw hundreds of seat cushions onto the pitch in protest at the inept Italian display. They, too, appreciated that Northern Ireland would be formidable opponents in Belfast, and the first of these Windsor Park fixtures was just a week away.

The game against Portugal in Belfast, to be played on Wednesday, 1 May, was the first occasion on which Northern Ireland had faced foreign opposition at home in a World Cup game. The display in Rome had clearly caught the imagination of the Ulster footballing public, and the match was now an all-ticket affair. It was a game everyone wanted to see, even though Northern Ireland had not won a match in two seasons. Nonetheless, like Jimmy McIlroy, the local football fans had been encouraged by what the team had achieved in the away games and believed this match could be won.

The visitors arrived in Belfast on the Monday before the contest. On the same night, indicative of an era when internationals were not allowed to interfere with domestic football, three of the Northern Ireland team were involved in club matches. For Jimmy McIlroy at Burnley, Bertie Peacock at Celtic, and Billy Simpson at Rangers it was business as usual. But at least Simpson got the fillip of a goal in his side's 4-3 defeat of Dunfermline.

Because the FA Cup final was just days away, the home team was again denied the services of Jackie Blanchflower and Peter McParland, Peter Doherty deciding to keep faith with the eleven men who had fought like gladiators in the Roman arena. In relation to the game in Lisbon back in January, Northern Ireland had three changes, but the Portuguese retained only five of the side from that first fixture. The teams were as follows:

Northern Ireland: Gregg (Doncaster Rovers); Cunningham (Leicester City), McMichael (Newcastle United); Blanchflower (Tottenham Hotspur), Cush (Glenavon), Casey (Newcastle United); Bingham (Sunderland), McIlroy (Burnley), Simpson (Rangers), McMorran (Doncaster Rovers), Peacock (Celtic).

Portugal: Gomes (Sporting Lisbon); Virgilio (FC Porto), Pires (Belenenses); Pedroto (FC Porto), Graca (Setebul), Cabrita (Covilha); Hernanai (FC Porto), Vasques (Sporting Lisbon), Aguas (Benfica), Salvador (Benfica), Cavem (Benfica).

The game was an evening kick-off, but some two-and-a-half hours earlier than the corresponding match in Lisbon. Windsor Park may not have been as large as the Alvalade Stadium, but the atmosphere matched anything a bigger ground could have produced. Fortunately, the home team matched the moment. From the outset, Northern Ireland looked sharper, quicker and more dangerous. The defence was rock solid, particularly McMichael who scarcely allowed the Portuguese right-winger Hernani a touch at the ball. Upon this foundation, Northern Ireland built an offensive strategy that pushed back the Portuguese. Bingham's game stuttered somewhat on the right of the attack, but Peacock was looking more comfortable on the left wing than he had in Rome as Northern Ireland seized the initiative.

Danny Blanchflower's passing, particularly his long, through balls, was at its best. Time and again he dissected the Portuguese midfield and defence, but the Northern Ireland forwards, McMorran especially, lacked the sharpness to exploit the opportunities created. The pressure on the Portuguese goal was nonetheless relentless, only Vasques providing occasional relief by sorties forward.

In the twenty-second minute, McIlroy was fouled about twenty-three yards from the Portuguese goal and a number of players hovered over the ball. It was Peacock who eventually took the kick, pushing it to Casey whose shot was an absolute piledriver, a goal all the way and nothing less than the team deserved.

Northern Ireland continued to dominate but were again frustrated by inaccurate marksmanship, McIlroy looking below par, and Bingham showing only flashes of what he was capable of. The half-time score of 1-0 was not a true reflection of the balance of play and as the second half progressed, Harry Gregg was little more than a spectator to the relentless onslaught on the Portuguese goal. Billy Simpson did put the ball in the Portuguese net but was adjudged to have been offside. Gregg must have begun to wonder if the forwards would ever be able to kill the match off when at last the breakthrough came. After sixty-one minutes a free-kick was awarded on the right, and from Cunningham's cross, centre-forward Billy Simpson soared majestically to head home the vital second goal.

The game was now surely won, but to their credit Northern Ireland continued to attack, bearing testimony to their manager's football philosophy. Their efforts did not go unrewarded. With about fifteen minutes left, McMorran burst through the left of the Portuguese defence and fired in a shot which Gomes handled uncertainly, the ball breaking free under the follow-up challenge of Billy Simpson. In a desperate attempt to retrieve the situation, the Portuguese 'keeper tried to push the ball to right-half Pedroto but McMorran intercepted and shot towards goal. And a goal it would have been but for Virgilio's dive and palm away. Today the right-back would have been sent off but a penalty-kick was not in dispute.

I am recounting this story just a few days after Robert Pires and Thierry Henry between them contrived to miss a penalty against Manchester City at Highbury, Pires' attempt to roll the ball to his colleague ending in a muddle and a free-kick to the defending side. Flashback to Windsor Park, 1 May 1957: Jimmy McIlroy steps up to take the penalty-kick but doesn't; at least he doesn't kick the ball at goal. If McIlroy is Pires, the Thierry Henry part is played by Danny Blanchflower – but to no greater effect. The Northern Ireland captain is adjudged to have encroached into the penalty area before McIlroy touched the ball. Although Blanchflower's shot finds the back of the net, the kick is ordered to be retaken. If only Pires and Henry had read their old copies of the *Belfast Telegraph*. Jimmy McIlroy recalls how that 'surprise move' originated:

> A day or two before the match, Danny came forward to Peter and he says, 'I'd like to work something if we get a penalty.' I would be taking the penalty, and the rest of the players would be outside the [eighteen-yard] box. As I bent down to place the ball on the spot ... I would just push it a yard to one side and Danny would come running and take the ball and dribble it past the 'keeper. Peter was petrified when he first heard of this

[responding] 'Why don't you just slam it into the net?' but Danny said, 'If we do something like this, we'll frighten the life out of them and they'll start wondering what's coming next.'

To say nothing of the 'wonder' among his own team-mates. McIlroy also argues that the referee's decision to have the penalty retaken was because he too was blinded by the 'wonder' of the moment: 'The referee had never seen [anything like] it before and his mind must have been puzzled, and he was standing beside me and he says, "I'd like you to take the penalty again," concluding 'This was the sort of person Danny was – he was full of ideas.'

It should be noted too that this Portugal match was not the only occasion on which McIlroy and Blanchflower shared a 'penalty moment', as McIlroy recollects:

I remember when we played Spurs in the [FA] Cup [final] at Wembley [in 1962], near the end Spurs got a penalty, and Danny, he took it. And he was setting the ball down, and placing it, and I was standing behind him ... trying to remember where Danny had placed the penalties before, and then I started to point to the [Burnley] 'keeper where he [Danny] was going to put it. Danny turned round and he saw me doing this and he said, 'Do you want to take the bloody thing?' ... Of course he stuck it in the net.

Back to Windsor Park in May 1957 – and that was precisely what McIlroy himself did with the retaken penalty, to give Northern Ireland a convincing 3-0 win, their first since beating Scotland at Windsor Park in October 1955 and the first time they had scored three goals at home since 1936 (when Wales had been beaten 3-2). Nonetheless, in contrast to the feelings almost of triumph after their 1-0 defeat in Rome, there was a sting in the victory over Portugal. It was not so much that they should have scored more goals – though that was certainly the case – it was more that the draw in Lisbon now looked like a point lost rather than a point gained. Yes, Northern Ireland were top of the group with three points from three games; but Italy stood ominously in second place with two points and having played two games less than Peter Doherty's side. The Italians were due to play Portugal at the end of the month and if they won that, they would be a point ahead of Northern Ireland with a game in hand. For most observers it was not so much a case of if they won but when they won, for on the strength of their two showings against the Ulstermen, Portugal had little hope of even scrambling a point against the Azurri.

Jimmy Greaves has famously described football as a 'funny old game', and the Portugal–Italy match on 26 May 1957 proved this conclusively. However, it could be argued that Portugal's 3-0 crushing of the Italians was not really a giant-killing act but a return to form by a side that had so far not lived up to its potential in this competition. For Northern Ireland, such debating points were irrelevant: all that mattered was that they now had a real chance of making it to the finals in Sweden. If Portugal failed to win in Italy and Northern Ireland could beat the Italians in Belfast, Doherty's 'glittering prize' would be theirs. The remaining matches were to be played in December. Would it be a winter of discontent or one made glorious summer? As they say in football, there was everything to play for.

Group 8 Table, end of May 1957

	P	W	D	L	F	A	Pts
N Ireland	3	1	1	1	4	2	3
Portugal	3	1	1	1	4	4	3
Italy	2	1	0	1	1	3	2

1. Northern Ireland v France, Festival of Britain match programme, 12 May 1951.
2. *Belfast Telegraph*, 14 January 1957.
3. Ibid.
4. Jimmy McIlroy, *Right Inside Soccer*, The Sportsman's Book Club, London, 1961, p. 20.
5. *Irish News*, 17 January 1957.
6. Ibid.
7. *Belfast Telegraph*, 25 April 1957.
8. Harry Gregg with Roger Anderson, *Harry's Game: The Autobiography*, Mainstream, 2002, p. 84.
9. *Belfast Telegraph*, 25 April 1957.
10. McIlroy, p.21.
11. *Belfast News-Letter*, 26 April 1957.
12. *Irish News*, 26 April 1957.
13. Ibid.

FOUR

THE BATTLE OF WINDSOR

Northern Ireland's all-important game against Italy, their last match in the qualifying group, was scheduled for 4 December 1957. Before that the team had two British Championship matches to play, against Scotland in Belfast and against England at Wembley exactly four weeks before the Italy fixture. The match with Scotland ended in a 1-1 draw but the real test for Doherty's side was the annual clash with England.

Despite the fact that Northern Ireland were facing an England team unbeaten in sixteen matches (including their last ten games at Wembley), and that they had not beaten England since 1927, and had only ever won once on English soil (in 1914), Peter Doherty's team approached the match believing that they could prevail.

The World Cup games had confirmed Northern Ireland's stature in international competition, as a team of talent and tenacity and, above all, a side that played to win. This may have been just their second visit to Wembley (the first, in 1955, ending in a 3-0 defeat), a venue usually reserved for foreign opposition and Scotland, but neither Peter Doherty nor his players were intimidated by the twin towers.

Doherty himself had graced Wembley in the first post-war cup final, and Jackie Blanchflower and Peter McParland had both starred there in the most recent final. For the likes of Danny Blanchflower and Jimmy McIlroy, Wembley's wide open spaces were the perfect stage to display their skills –

which is exactly what they did. (Arguably, the irrepressible Gerry Morgan was even less in awe of the arena. When the Northern Ireland team and IFA officials inspected the pitch before the game, some of the selectors and others remarked on how great it was for their team to have an opportunity to play on such a stage, to which Gerry responded, 'Great my arse – the dogs have been running here for a hundred years!')

England's dangerman had been identified as Johnny Haynes but the tactics devised to nullify this threat did not seem to be working. In response, and providing a perfect illustration of the Doherty–Blanchflower partnership, the Northern Ireland captain took the initiative to personally shadow the England playmaker, thereby neutralising Haynes and allowing Northern Ireland to take the offensive. Jimmy McIlroy gave the visitors the lead from the penalty spot – somewhat fortuitously it must be said, after his shot hit the post but cannoned off the despairing England 'keeper Eddie Hopkinson and across the goal-line – and Northern Ireland went in at half-time 1-0 up.

Although Harry Gregg was giving a re-run of his Rome performance, England managed to break through thirteen minutes into the second half, Alan A'Court making the score 1-1. England, in truth, were making plenty of chances but the twin strike force of Tommy Taylor and Derek Kevan could not provide the killer finish.

Northern Ireland redoubled their efforts, Jackie Blanchflower and Bertie Peacock both taking on man-marking roles to stifle England's creativity and give the initiative back to the visitors. In the sixty-seventh minute Northern Ireland regained the lead, the unlikely marksman being the debutant from Third Division Southend United, Sammy McCrory, one of the oldest players on the field. Scarcely before England had recovered their composure, Northern Ireland made it 3-1, Billy Simpson diving to head in Bingham's cross.

England now unleashed an all-out assault on Harry Gregg's goal but although Duncan Edwards reduced the arrears, Northern Ireland held on, inspired in particular by Gregg, Peacock and the Blanchflower brothers, the first team to beat England at the famous stadium since Hungary in November 1953. When the final whistle sounded, Wembley belonged to the men in green.

Interviewed after the match, England manager Walter Winterbottom described Northern Ireland, at least on this occasion, as a lucky team, to which Danny Blanchflower responded in his post-match interview that 'I'd rather be a lucky team than a good team.' Of course he did not really mean it, nor was it a fair appraisal of Doherty's side.

On an individual level, Harry Gregg was shortly to be rewarded with a transfer from Doncaster Rovers to Manchester United (after the Italy game on 4 December) while Wilbur Cush was soon to move from Glenavon to Leeds United. But as a team, the 3-2 defeat of England, their first for thirty years, putting them top of the British Championship table, was a massive psychological boost for Northern Ireland as they prepared to meet Italy at Windsor Park, just a few weeks away.

The travelling show that was the Italian international football team arrived in Belfast on Sunday, 1 December, three days before the big game. Including eighteen players and manager Dr Alphonse Foni (a member of Italy's World Cup winning side of 1938), together with support staff, officials of the Federazione Italiana Guioco Calcio (FIGC or Italian Football Federation) and journalists, there was a total of forty-four people making up the party. This was big-time football the like of which Northern Ireland had not seen before.

Of course Italy offered not only quantity but crucially quality as well. Two players in particular, who had not featured in the Rome match in April, caught the public's attention.

Right-winger Alcide Ghiggia and inside-right Juan Schiaffino were both former Uruguayan internationals now playing in Italy and qualifying for the international side as naturalised Italians. Not only were they Uruguayan internationals but they were the players who had scored the goals that defeated Brazil in the Maracana Stadium in 1950 to bring the World Cup back to Montevideo.

Four years later, Tommy Docherty got a close up view of Schiaffino when Scotland faced Uruguay in the 1954 World Cup finals in Switzerland: his verdict was that the South American was the finest inside-forward he had ever encountered. Doherty's assessment was obviously shared by AC Milan who were prepared to pay £75,000 to secure Schiaffino's services. Now Schiaffino and Ghiggia, along with another South American, Michelangelo Montuori, were set to provide perhaps Northern Ireland's most formidable test ever in international football.

Despite Northern Ireland's commendable performance in Rome and the recent victory at Wembley, they were still very much underdogs against the Azurri. The Italian press were generally of the opinion that the team chosen to play at Windsor Park was much stronger than that which won the first game (only four of whom retained their place). And as to the possibility of a Northern Ireland victory, one member of the Italian press corps spoke for his nation: 'Italy's soccer public will not hear of defeat. Should it happen, the effect would be tantamount to an earthquake or other national disaster.' But the team which had won the World Cup in 1934 and 1938 and had appeared in all of the final tournaments did not expect an earthquake as they went through their preparations at Cliftonville's Solitude ground.

At least Northern Ireland would be at full strength – or almost. First-choice centre-forward Billy Simpson, scorer of the third goal against England, had picked up an injury in a European Cup game at Ibrox Park the previous week.

Ironically Rangers' opponents on that occasion had been AC Milan who had two representatives in the Italian side at Windsor Park. Simpson's replacement was to be Billy McAdams of Manchester City. The teams who were to battle it out for a place in the World Cup finals were the following:

Northern Ireland: Gregg (Doncaster Rovers); Keith (Newcastle United), McMichael (Newcastle United); Blanchflower, D (Tottenham Hotspur), Blanchflower, J (Manchester United), Peacock (Celtic); Bingham (Sunderland), McIlroy (Burnley), McAdams (Manchester City), Cush (Leeds United), McParland (Aston Villa).

Italy: Bugatti (Napoli); Corradi (Juventus), Cervato (Fiorentina); Chiapella (Fiorentina), Ferrario (Juventus), Segato (Fiorentina); Ghiggia (Roma), Schiaffino (AC Milan), Bean (AC Milan), Gratton (Fiorentina), Montuori (Fiorentina).

As far as I am aware, the Italian centre-forward had no connection to the Rowan Atkinson character. In any event, the stage was set and the actors were ready, but the drama was to begin long before kick-off.

The match officials assigned to this crucial World Cup qualifier were all Hungarian: Franz Viragg and Alex Haraniozos running the line (today's assistant referees) and Istvan Zsolt the referee. (Northern Ireland had canvassed for a British referee for this match but the Italians were insistent that a continental European be appointed – and FIFA made the judgement in Italy's favour.) When he was not acting as the man in the middle in international football contests, Zsolt was the stage manager of the Budapest Opera House, a man with a busy schedule. However, life was going to get a lot busier for him when faced by what amounted to a flying marathon to get him from Budapest to Belfast. The journey had no fewer than four legs – Budapest to Prague;

Prague to Brussels; Brussels to London; and finally, London to Belfast (or to be more precise – and one can only wonder what foreign visitors made of the name – Nutt's Corner), ETA Tuesday night, match day minus one.

But even before Zsolt took to the air, a glitch occurred. By the Monday before the game, the referee and his linesmen had still not received their British visas. The Hungarian FA now contacted Billy Drennan at the IFA to see if he could give the system a push, which he duly did by in turn contacting his opposite number at the FA in London, Sir Stanley Rous. Sir Stanley was indeed the right man to engage and soon the Foreign Office were, I suppose we could say, 'on the ball' and the visas on the way.

As to the journey itself, all went swimmingly – or should that be flyingly? – as far as Brussels, but then our perennial friend the British weather intervened. London was fogbound and Mr Zsolt's plane had to divert to an airfield in Kent. The net result was that he failed to make his connection with the plane to Belfast – the 'Ulster Flyer' as it was known. Still, all was not lost and arrangements were made for the Hungarian party to fly to Northern Ireland at eight o'clock the next morning, 4 December, the day of the game. This was a perfectly feasible re-scheduling, but it depended on the fog having cleared – and it did not. A Wagnerian drama, worthy no doubt of the opera house in Budapest, had just begun.

The flight that should have taken Zsolt to Nutt's Corner (later Belfast International Airport) was cancelled but the hope was that the fog would lift, allowing the Hungarian to catch a later plane. An alternative was to drive to Birmingham and fly from there at 2.00 pm but the fog ruled out progress by road as well. Italian officials in Belfast, led by the president of the FIGC, Dr Ottorino Barassi, now appraised of the situation by their IFA counterparts, were prepared to have the kick-off delayed and play under the Windsor Park floodlights if the afternoon light began to fail in order to give Zsolt every chance to reach Belfast. Working on his own initiative, IFA Secretary Billy Drennan made contingency plans for the English international referee Arthur Ellis to travel by train to Stranraer and then catch the ferry to Larne. The Italians, however, were adamant that it was Zsolt or no one, so the waiting game continued. The delay proved fatal to both options – Zsolt or Ellis as referee – leaving the parties with a most unsatisfactory 'Plan C': an Ulster referee taking charge. The Italian response to that one did not need a translator.

The fact that this World Cup fixture could have been refereed by Arthur Ellis provides a fascinating pause for thought for those of my generation for whom the name Arthur Ellis will always be linked with the BBC's classic *It's a Knockout* series of the 1970s. Ellis, who was referee (what else?) on the show, shared the stage with two other sporting greats: Eddie 'Up 'n' Under' Waring and Stuart Hall, whose infectious laughter will be forever etched on my mind. Ah, nostalgia. But wait, what was happening back in Belfast on 4 December 1957?

The answer was, to borrow from Paul Daniels, 'not a lot'. The IFA and FIGC delegations were at loggerheads over what to do. It should be pointed out that on 4 December there were in fact two contests between Italy and Northern Ireland: the football match at Windsor Park, and preceding it at the Midland Hotel, a match of football politics between the respective governing bodies which kicked off at approximately 12.20 pm. The Italians, appropriately enough, played a defensive game, rejecting the Ellis option and that of a local referee. By this stage it was obvious that Zsolt was not going to make it but Billy Drennan did not want to cancel the game as it was far too late to issue such a notice – fans were already Windsor Park-bound from all over Northern Ireland.

The suggestion that the game be played as a friendly was probably Drennan's, but when the meeting broke up at 12.55

pm no firm decision had been taken although a provisional agreement had been drafted. The two sides were to reconvene at Windsor Park at 1.45 pm and when they did (although it was nearer 1.55 pm due to the Italians being late), it was agreed to put the draft into effect.

The piece of paper signed by Dr Barassi on behalf of the FIGC and Joseph McBride as president of the IFA, and witnessed by the Lord Mayor of Belfast, Sir Cecil McKee, had two principal clauses. Firstly, the match at Windsor Park was reclassified as a friendly, and a return friendly game was to be played in Italy on a date to be arranged. The second clause stated that the World Cup qualifier would be played in Belfast at a date to be agreed by the IFA and the FIGC.

Superficially this may have appeared as a cave-in by the IFA, which would have fitted an apparent recent pattern of letting the Italians have their way, for example in agreeing that the first group match between the two be played in Italy and that the return fixture be played midweek rather than a Saturday and in daylight rather than under floodlights. However, a Windsor Park friendly was in fact a compromise by the Italians – their preference would have been to simply cancel the match and head home. It was only after IFA appeals that around 50,000 people were on their way to the ground that Dr Barassi and his colleagues shifted their position. The referee for the friendly was confirmed as Tommy Mitchell from Lurgan. It was probably a relief to all concerned that a reasonably amicable settlement had been reached; if so, it was a relief that was to be short-lived.

Peter McParland vividly recalls hearing the news about the changed circumstances surrounding the World Cup 'qualifier':

> We were all changing in the dressing room ... with about twenty minutes [to go] you're getting the final preparations ... you're all worked up for the game. Peter

The battle of Windsor

[Doherty] walked in and said, 'I've got some news for you boys ... the World Cup match is off, but we're going to play them in a friendly game.' It was a big, big knock-back that that happened.

McParland has no complaints about Italy's stance on the question of the referee – 'Well, you can't blame them ... we wouldn't have wanted a bloody Italian [in charge] out there [for the game in Rome]' – but at the same time acknowledges that the Northern Ireland team were aggrieved that the game they had been so eagerly awaiting was to be denied them. 'It was a hell of a knock-back from standing there, sitting there, waiting to go out and play the most important World Cup game.'

Windsor Park was packed to capacity, the crowd figure somewhere in the region of 50,000. Many had taken a half-day or full-day off work, eagerly anticipating a match of a stature unparalleled in the annals of Northern Ireland football. The fans were of course oblivious to all the behind-the-scenes developments of that morning: they had come to Windsor Park to see their team take on the twice world champions and hopefully see them triumph. They were totally unprepared for the news from the public address system.

Billy Drennan's announcement was honest but hardly discreet. He told the Windsor Park crowd that the match referee had been detained by fog in London and since the Italians would not accept a local referee officiating in a World Cup game, the match had been re-classified as a friendly. Shock quickly turned to anger and fury among the spectators who vented their frustration on the teams when they appeared. The jeers and boos which greeted the players continued throughout the playing of the Italian national anthem (but stopped while 'The Queen' was played), a matter which would create some controversy in the light of subsequent events and an issue to which we will return.

The mood off the pitch was ugly and intimidating by kick-off time and was undoubtedly a factor in what was to happen on the pitch. Whether the Italians were truly incensed by the lack of respect accorded to their national anthem or felt threatened by the hostile atmosphere in the ground, the play deteriorated into what can only be described as a brutal affair.

The game was a tinderbox waiting only for a spark to set it on fire and Billy McAdams's shoulder charge on Bugatti duly incensed the Italians, who did not hold anything back in their response. First Bingham was felled by left-back Cervato, then Wilbur Cush was sent tumbling from a crude tackle by Schiaffino which ripped the Lurgan man's shin pad. Cush, seething, showed the damage to team-mate McParland: 'Look at that … I'll give him something in a minute.' Not one prone to turn the other cheek, 'wee Wilbur' bided his time and then thundered into the former Uruguayan international in a real bone crusher of a challenge. Observing the duel – if that is the right word – Jimmy McIlroy remarks, 'Instead of feeling sorry for Wilbur, I began to feel sorry for the Italian.'

The Italians were particularly sensitive about challenges on their 'keeper and when a goalmouth mêlée ensued following a Peter McParland attempt to unsettle Bugatti, revenge was exacted on Billy McAdams for his early encounter with the 'keeper. In the scramble, Chiapella, the Italian right-half, thrust his knees into McAdams's back when the latter stumbled over Bugatti. It was an outrageous challenge that left Tommy Mitchell with no option but to send off the Italian. Even though only two minutes of the game was left at this point, Chiapella was reluctant to go, eventually persuaded to do so by his own officials. This was one of the few correct decisions made by the Lurgan referee for in truth he had lost control of the game at an early stage and never really regained it. McParland recalls how he set off that chain of events:

> I went in on the 'keeper and hit him. Then half the Italians were after me, and I wouldn't turn round ... I kept walking away because I would've got a box in the mouth or be in the middle of it ... And Billy McAdams was pulling them or pushing them out of the way. One fellow [Chiapella] made a lunge with his boot at me.

Symptomatic of a match where discipline had totally disappeared was the performance of the Italian centre-half Rino Ferrario who seemed to kick anything that moved. Billy Bingham recounted one incident arising out of a Northern Ireland corner:

> McIlroy and I took up position near the far post, and as soon as McParland put his foot to the corner-kick, Ferrario, the Italian centre-half, let out a Tarzan yell and jumped at both of us with his feet. For this offence we were given an indirect free-kick![2]

Ferrario should of course have played no further part in the game but Tommy Mitchell lacked the courage and composure to bring the Italians into line. Instead, they continued to run rampant. Danny Blanchflower had some sympathy for the referee's wariness at provoking total pandemonium if he took tough action against the visitors. The Northern Ireland captain had to suffer his own share of provocation from the Italians, Chiapella even landing a punch on Blanchflower's chin early on, but he did what he could to diffuse a game that was getting uglier by the minute. When Northern Ireland were awarded a penalty and Ferrario refused to hand over the ball, Blanchflower persuaded the referee to change his decision to a free-kick. Discretion may have been the better part of valour in this instance but what credibility did the referee have when he allowed players to make his decisions?

No Northern Ireland player was spared the rough-house tactics. When a free-kick was awarded to the home side just outside the Italian penalty area, Danny Blanchflower told Billy Bingham to insert himself in the defensive wall and 'shake them up'. Bingham followed his captain's orders but soon found himself 'shook up' and sprawling at Blanchflower's feet. 'You get in the ****ing wall,' Bingham suggested, but Danny stayed put.

Almost forgotten amidst the frenzy and the fouls was that some good football had also been played, remarkably enough. Northern Ireland had controlled the opening encounters, but had found Bugatti in inspired form in the Italian goal, much as his opposite number Harry Gregg had been in Rome. Against the run of play, however, it was the visitors who broke the deadlock, Montuori slipping a pass to Ghiggia in the inside-left position, from which the South American struck the ball cleanly past Gregg in the twenty-third minute. Northern Ireland responded within four minutes, Bingham working the ball to the by-line and pulling it back for Cush to equalise.

The score remained level until half-time but now the artistry of the Italians was beginning to exert itself, Ghiggia and Montuori displaying their talents as exponents of cultured attacking play. The two had combined for Ghiggia's goal, and seven minutes into the second half Montuori rounded off a delightful passing move to put Italy back in front. Again, Northern Ireland came back. Peacock forced a magnificent save from Bugatti with a shot bound for the top right-hand corner, and then in the fifty-ninth minute an attack down the left ended with the diminutive Cush crashing home his and his team's second goal.

With Jackie Blanchflower a towering presence in the home defence, and Bugatti continuing to handle well, there was no further scoring. The physical edge to the game, however, remained keen, and more than that at times, and the final whistle, unfortunately, did not signal an end to hostilities.

The Northern Ireland fans had suffered a collective wound when the decision to play the game as a friendly had been announced; the antics of the Italian team over the course of the match had rubbed salt into that wound and then squeezed it in a vice. The referee's whistle brought a pitch invasion by the crowd and inevitably more trouble.

Billy Bingham had gone to shake hands with the man who had had no hesitation in committing one cynical foul after another on him during the game, left-back Cervato. The Northern Ireland outside-right noticed what he at first thought were autograph hunters also approaching the Italian but quickly realised that their intentions were not so benign. He recalled: 'So instead of letting go of Cervato's hand, I held on to it tightly and tugged him towards the safety of the dressing rooms. We sprinted all the way, with Cervato ducking punches and jinking round kicks.'[3]

Meanwhile, Harry Gregg had to come to the rescue of Bean of AC Milan:

> I heard him crying and went over. I put my arm around his shoulder, thinking that would be enough to protect him. Then an arm came over my shoulder and whacked him with a stone. Down he went, and in the spur of the moment I began laying into anything that moved. I kicked and punched until the police arrived on the scene. Bene [Bean] was eventually returned to his teammates, who by this stage were standing on the benches and hanging on to the window ledge of their dressing-room. They thought we'd done the damage to their player and I decided it best not to wait around to explain.[4]

(I can't help wondering how Peter McParland's shoulder charging incident in the 1957 FA Cup final might have developed if the Manchester United 'keeper had been Harry Gregg instead of Ray Wood.) Not all the Italian players surrendered themselves to this post-match fate, as Danny Blanchflower witnessed.

When the game ended he recalled instructing his players to each escort an Italian player to safety, an order that may have been garbled or drowned out by the uproar in the crowd. In any event, he attached himself to Rino Ferrario, one of the chief culprits in an afternoon of serial fouling, but as they headed for the dressing rooms the crowd engulfed them:

> As we reached the halfway line on our way from the field Ferrario suddenly let out a fierce scream and clutched at his kidneys. As I was walking beside him I do not know what had happened behind. He might have been struck a sharp blow; he might have mistaken a friendly thump on the back for one; I do not know. After his agonised scream he turned on a fellow in an overcoat who had his hands in his pocket and attacked him. He punched the overcoated figure in the stomach and as it doubled up he struck it to the ground with a fierce blow on the head. Then he belted into the crumpled figure with both fists giving it a real hiding.[5]

The word mayhem scarcely does justice to the scenes at Windsor Park as the two teams struggled to get off the pitch amidst an invading crowd of two thousand or more. The police were unprepared for the violence and were slow to respond: it could be argued that the pre-match atmosphere and events on the field should have inspired vigilance in preparing to police the post-match situation but the resources and reaction proved totally inadequate. The fact that only one man was arrested and charged – a Scot, Thomas Murphy, now living in Belfast who was later fined £5 for disorderly conduct and assaulting a policeman – was a statistic that spoke for itself.

The IFA prohibited Doherty or any of his players from talking to the press afterwards and Italian officials also declined to comment to reporters. The only official announcement came from Billy Drennan, stating simply that the fixture would be on the agenda at the next meeting of the Association.

Although tempers had cooled by the time of the post-match banquet in the evening – some of the Italians even expressing remorse to their Northern Ireland counterparts for their excesses during the game – there would undoubtedly be repercussions from the day's events. The players, in the end, may have emerged none the worse for wear, but the Italian press was another matter.

The correspondent of the communist newspaper *L'Unita* described Windsor Park as 'a scene of collective hysteria, a scene of unchained fury'[6] while the Rome paper *Il Messagero* was no less emotive:

> It was a scene of savagery and unbelievable cowardice …
> Seen from the stands, the blue figure of one of the Italian players emerged occasionally from the howling mob of 3,000 people, intent on beating them up.[7]

Little wonder that with this style of reporting, questions were even raised about the affair in the Italian parliament. Speakers in both the Senate and lower house pressed Prime Minister Zoli to send an official protest to Northern Ireland about the way their players had been treated and the Italian national anthem dishonoured. The government, however, was in no hurry to escalate the matter and responded by informing parliament that they would await a report from the Italian National Olympic Committee.

Questions were also asked about the affair in the Northern Ireland Parliament at Stormont, most of them from the Independent Belfast MP Frank Hanna. Responding, the Minister for Home Affairs Walter Topping did not accept the contentions that the Italian anthem had been dishonoured or that, more questionably, the police arrangements had been unsatisfactory. Both in Italy and Northern Ireland then, government was essentially unmoved by the 'Battle of Windsor'.

The IFA, however, could not afford to be inactive, especially as Italy was expected to raise the Windsor Park episode with FIFA. So, the IFA met on 10 December, six days after the match, and drew up a draft report for world football's governing body. It was also anticipated that referee Tommy Mitchell would submit his own report to FIFA. These were worrying times for the Irish Football Association because it was not beyond the realms of possibility that FIFA would order the World Cup fixture to be played at a neutral venue or, even worse, allow the 2-2 draw to stand as a World Cup result because of the fear of further trouble at a rearranged match in Belfast, as the *Northern Whig* newspaper speculated.

Then, surely and perceptibly, the mood began to change. The attack on the IFA and the Windsor Park fans began to relent, the tide of abuse started to ebb and even flow in Northern Ireland's favour. Now, a more objective view of what had happened at Windsor Park on 4 December began to emerge. For example, the former Scottish international 'keeper Jack Harkness, writing in the *Sunday Post*, dealt directly with the alleged dishonouring of the Italian national anthem which had supposedly provoked the Italian team into an ill-disciplined display in the game itself:

> Well, I was one of the crowd, I heard no Italian Anthem being played. The band could have been playing 'Tiger Rag' for all we knew. Because at that time the crowd were STILL jeering, hissing, and booing the announcement about the game being a friendly.
> In fact, as far as I can see, the Italians are deliberately making martyrs of themselves to cover up the lack of

sportsmanship of their officials OFF the field and several of their players ON the field.

Their one solitary complaint is with the break-in [pitch invasion] after the game when I consider the police were slow in getting off their marks.

They should ask themselves this: – Had the same last-minute announcement been made in Rome, Milan, Florence, or Turin, how would Italian spectators have reacted [?]

So let sympathy be directed to the Italians solely for the lack of protection the players received going off the field. But none for any of the events that took place before or during the actual game.[8]

Harkness's view was supported by two Irishmen of Italian extraction – cousins Frank Forte from Belfast and Romeo Forte from Armagh – who sent the following letter to the leading newspapers in Rome, Milan and Naples:

As Irish-born Italians we feel that we should defend the honour and dignity of our numerous Irish friends by bringing to your notice views other than those expressed by the Italian Press and radio. The Press have, in our opinion, been misleading.

The main body of the spectators were workers who had forfeited their day's wages, as well as the entrance fee, to see a football match of World Cup status. The crowd felt that they were justified in showing deep resentment when it turned out to be merely a friendly game.

The first misunderstanding occurred when the Italian Anthem was being played. It was not audible or recognisable above the unabated clamour except by those in the immediate vicinity of the band.

The jeering and booing was directed solely against the gross mis-management of the controlling bodies concerned. The majority of the crowd which invaded the field were only seeking autographs from both teams. This is verified by the news-reels.

The regrettable incidents which then occurred would surely never have been allowed to develop had the police on duty expected any such disgraceful conduct as that complained of. Their laxity can better be understood than excused.

Our greatest admiration goes to the Irish players, especially Gregg, Blanchflower and Cush, who did everything possible on their own initiative and at personal risk to protect their guests. Let us not allow ourselves to brand any country or people on the hooliganism of a few irresponsibles.

We hope that any grievance, real or imaginary, will be forgiven and forgotten by both parties. Let us, as true sportsmen, shake hands in good-will so that friendship and the true spirit of sport may prevail.[9]

Although we cannot quantify their impact, such sentiments seemed to bear fruit, for on 13 December, just nine days after the game, *Reuters* news agency reported that the Italians were prepared to return to Belfast and honour their agreement to play the World Cup fixture provided that all reasonable measures were taken to protect their players. Two days later, FIFA's World Cup organising committee met in Zurich but by all accounts the Windsor Park affair – including the report from the IFA and any report from the FIGC that may have been presented – was not even raised.

The position taken by Italy's government was in fact an indication that saner counsel had prevailed over the furore created by the press. Dr Barassi, the president of the Federazione Italiana Guioco Calcio, was not prepared to breach the agreement made with the IFA that the World Cup qualifier would be played in Belfast in January.

So, FIFA took no action and accepted the arrangements that the IFA and FIGC had made to replay the game. No sanctions were imposed on either side in view of all the circumstances surrounding the game on 4 December. Some Northern Ireland fans blamed their own football authorities for making the fateful announcement just minutes before the kick-off, incensing a crowd who were anticipating a World Cup decider. The IFA response to this charge, reasonably enough, was that the timing of the announcement was dictated by the fact that a final agreement with the Italians was only reached at the eleventh hour. Northern Ireland were, however, fortunate not to be punished for what happened once the game ended, and IFA President Joe McBride's contention that the whole affair was the responsibility of those who failed to get Zsolt and party to Belfast in time simply looked like trying to pass the buck.

Billy Bingham has a different analysis of the whole affair, focusing on the mental attitude of the Italians before the game and their inability to cope with the atmosphere at Windsor Park during the game: 'The Italians came thinking, "We're going to kick the shit out of them." That's the way they felt … they were a little bit apprehensive because the Irish … are resilient and tough … The crowd [also] got them going. I don't think they'd faced that animosity before.' That support had a positive effect on the home team. 'I think it gives you momentum,' continues Bingham, 'the fact that the crowd are so serious about wanting you to win. It gets to you.'

As far as the Northern Ireland players were concerned, they had proved to themselves that they could beat Italy, although that was not Jimmy McIlroy's initial response: 'I remember coming off the field thinking, "This is some team we're playing," and I had doubts about beating them. And yet Danny Blanchflower, speaking to him afterwards … said, "After that game, I'm certain we can beat them." … That bucked me up a lot, to hear Danny say something like that.'

If Northern Ireland had taken the penalty awarded, the final score might well have been 3-2 in their favour. At that stage, of course, a victory would not have guaranteed qualification because Portugal could still have ended level on points if they had beaten Italy in their last game (requiring then a play-off match since neither goal average nor goal difference was to count in terms of the final placings). The postponement of the World Cup clash to January 1958 removed this degree of uncertainty because the Italy–Portugal match was to be played in Milan on 22 December. Evidently carrying no scars, physical or psychological, from the Belfast encounter, Italy ran out comfortable winners, 3-0, ending Portuguese hopes. The group table, with one game left, meant that to qualify for Sweden, Italy had only to draw; Northern Ireland had to win.

Group Table after game on 22 December 1957

	P	W	D	L	F	A	Pts
Italy	3	2	0	1	4	3	4
N Ireland	3	1	1	1	4	2	3
Portugal	4	1	1	2	4	7	3

And so Italy came back to Belfast on Sunday, 12 January 1958, three days before the match that would decide who went to Sweden. The bus journey from Nutt's Corner to Belfast took almost an hour due to snow on the roads but the team and officials quickly settled into the familiar surroundings of the Midland Hotel. President of the FIGC Dr Barassi certainly appeared upbeat in his comments to the press: 'We are glad to be back in Belfast ... I believe we shall get a sporting reception on Wednesday.'[10]

On the same day most of the Northern Ireland squad assembled at the Strand Hotel in Portstewart. The party included the reserves Norman Uprichard and Derek Dougan of Portsmouth and Jackie Scott of Grimsby. Absent were

Harry Gregg and Jackie Blanchflower of Manchester United, Alfie McMichael of Newcastle United and Aston Villa's Peter McParland. McMichael was due to arrive on Monday, McParland on Tuesday after playing for Aston Villa in a FA Cup third round replay against Stoke City at Molineux (which as it turned out, Villa lost 2-0).

Blanchflower's and Gregg's absence was explained by Manchester United's European Cup quarter-final against Red Star Belgrade, to be played at Old Trafford on the Tuesday night. It was arranged that Gregg, who would be playing against Red Star, would take a taxi from Manchester to Heysham and then sail to Belfast. Blanchflower had lost his first-team place to Mark Jones but had to stay in Manchester to await the outcome of a fitness test on Jones. When the latter was passed fit to play, Blanchflower joined the Northern Ireland team on Tuesday.

Important early arrivals for the match also included the Hungarian officials who had missed the original encounter. On this occasion nothing was left to chance: Zsolt and his colleagues travelled by train from Budapest to Vienna, then flew to London to connect with the 'Ulster Flyer' and arrived in Belfast on Sunday evening, 12 January. (Apparently Zsolt had had to leave rehearsals for *Peer Gynt* at a crucial stage, but at least he would be back in plenty of time for the first public performance on 3 February.) No escapades with fog this time, or so everyone thought at this point.

The game came at a difficult time for Northern Ireland manager Peter Doherty, who was involved in a dispute with one of the directors of Doncaster Rovers, Hubert Bates. Both sides were taking legal advice and there was even press speculation that Doherty was about to move to the vacant manager's job at Bristol City. All very unsettling in the build-up to the biggest game in Northern Ireland's football history.

By contrast, the mood in the Italian camp appeared relaxed. Their players were on an £800 per man bonus if they qualified for the World Cup, a figure that dwarfed the £50 fee for each of the Northern Ireland players, irrespective of the result. On just six per cent of the Italians' potential earnings, Peter Doherty's men were certainly not playing for the money but then neither were their opponents. They had a self-assurance born of past international successes (including never having failed to qualify for the World Cup finals) and now they were just one point away from qualifying for the finals in Sweden. Well might the team take some time off from the match preparations to go shopping and sightseeing in Belfast city centre on the Monday. All seemed well with Dr Foni's side.

That was certainly the impression Italy wanted to give, but behind the confident exterior lurked some serious concerns. Three of the side that had played in Belfast in December were ruled out of this game through injury or illness: left-back and captain Sergio Cervato (the scorer of the goal that had beaten Northern Ireland in Rome the previous April); right-half Giuseppe Chiapella (who had been sent off in the December contest); and, most seriously, inside-forward and playmaker Guido Gratton. Gratton's place was to be taken by the Brazilian, now naturalised Italian, Dino Da Costa, one of four South Americans in the team (the others being Ghiggia, Schiaffino and Montuori). In addition, centre-forward Gaston Bean was out of favour and was replaced by Guido Pivatelli of Bologna (who had played against Portugal in Milan and was in fact the only Italian-born player in Italy's forward line). Dr Barassi had to acknowledge to reporters that having six changes in the team from the previous game in Belfast was not what the Italians would have wished for:

> We had had a bit of bad luck having to resort to substitutions of injured players, and the situation is as a result more difficult than we expected.
>
> The changes in line-up will create difficulties for us in the

technique of play we had planned for the game. Now we are going to have to improvise a bit.[11]

The Northern Ireland line-up, if anything, was stronger for this match. True, Dick Keith was an injury loss at right-back, but his replacement, Willie Cunningham, was a vastly experienced and reliable performer; while the return of Billy Simpson at centre-forward in place of Billy McAdams promised more potency in attack. Psychologically then, the initiative may have rested with Northern Ireland, and Doherty deliberately kept the build-up to the game as low-key as possible, with a game of golf on the Monday and only light practice on the Tuesday. On the night before the game, the team were the guests of the local cinema in Coleraine to watch a film of their recent triumph over England. The Italians, meanwhile, again went through their paces at Solitude.

Low-key was not how one would have described the public mood as the day of the match approached. Arguably, interest in this game was even more intense than for the original Belfast encounter, no doubt influenced by all the controversy surrounding the 'Battle of Windsor'. The rumour mill was working overtime, one story having the referee again withdrawing from the event, this time due to influenza. Zsolt, however, appeared in Belfast on Monday to reassure all concerned that he had no intention of missing what he described as 'the most important match of my life'.[12]

Two hundred telephone lines were installed at Windsor Park to accommodate the international press coverage while the BBC was also due to televise the game (apart from, for some reason, the opening ten minutes), the first ever live broadcast of a football match in Ireland. The commentator was to be Kenneth Wolstenholme, later to become famous as the early voice of *Match of the Day* and for the 'they think it's all over' remark as Geoff Hurst completed his hat-trick in the 1966 World Cup final. Broadcast rights had been secured for what the *Belfast Telegraph* referred to in typical jargon as 'a substantial fee'.[13] There was also to be a more substantial police presence at this match, with some two dozen RUC officers to patrol inside the stadium, supported by others on standby both inside and outside the ground. Everyone was ready for a great drama and, as on 4 December, it began early.

Harry Gregg, it will be remembered, was playing for Manchester United against Red Star Belgrade on the Tuesday night, a game, incidentally, that United won 3-2. He was then to take a taxi to the Heysham boat. However, a later than originally planned kick-off in the European tie meant the Heysham option was no longer viable. Instead, Gregg was now to fly from Manchester's Ringway Airport at 9.30 on the Wednesday morning, destination Nutt's Corner. And so in Manchester, Wednesday morning dawned … foggy. It was a re-run of the Zsolt affair but with Harry Gregg in the starring role. Suddenly Peter Doherty's careful pre-match build-up was thrown into confusion. The fog did not lift and the second-choice 'keeper Norman Uprichard was in the team, the Portsmouth player made aware of the fact as the team were travelling to Belfast from the north coast. He remembers that they had stopped in Ballymena for some refreshment and Peter Doherty had pulled him aside. 'Norman,' he said quite calmly, 'you're in.' And where did this leave team morale? They would not have to wait long for an answer.

And what of Harry Gregg? Well, he ended up watching the game on TV in the terminal building at Ringway Airport. Indeed, all eyes were now on Windsor Park.

The last-minute change to Peter Doherty's team meant that Northern Ireland and Italy fielded the following sides:

Northern Ireland: Uprichard (Portsmouth); Cunningham (Leicester City), McMichael (Newcastle Utd); Blanchflower,

D (Tottenham Hotspur), Blanchflower, J (Manchester Utd),
Peacock (Celtic); Bingham (Sunderland), Cush (Leeds Utd),
Simpson (Rangers), McIlroy (Burnley), McParland (Aston
Villa).

Italy: Bugatti (Napoli); Vincenzi (Inter Milan), Corradi
(Juventus); Invernezzi (Inter Milan), Ferrario (Juventus),
Segato (Fiorentina); Ghiggia (Roma), Schiaffino (AC Milan),
Pivatelli (Bologna), Montuori (Fiorentina), Da Costa (Roma).

Despite the eleventh-hour glitch, Northern Ireland were
ready for the challenge. 'We were more secure in the second
game,' claims Bingham, thanks to the showing in the first
match. Doherty's instructions were to 'Hit them hard – fairly,
but hard. Don't argue with them.' Discipline, strength and
skill were the order of the day.

As to the crowd, they were on their best behaviour,
remaining silent during the playing of the Italian national
anthem, even applauding some of the fine play that the
visitors exhibited during the game. Most importantly, there
was no attempt to encroach on the field of play at any stage
(a public announcement before the game had confirmed that
this would not be tolerated). The focus was now back where
it should have been – on the match itself.

Although masters of the defensive game, Italy gave no
signs of playing for a draw, first Ghiggia setting up debutant
Da Costa to shoot wide and then Schiaffino posing a threat,
prompting his fellow forwards and probing the Northern
Ireland defence. Northern Ireland also attacked with vigour
but McParland's shot after five minutes did not trouble
Bugatti, and the Italian 'keeper also saved comfortably from
McMichael's long-range effort.

While McParland did not really test the Italian 'keeper
with that effort, he does remember being tested himself early
on: 'Their left-back started at right-back ... and somebody
played one in the air to me and [smacking one hand against

the other for emphasis] he came in not any way thinking "I'll play the ball" [but rather] he's going to hammer me.'

Bingham and Cush then pressed on the right, exchanging passes and setting up Peacock but again the shot missed the target. The best of the early Northern Ireland attacks was probably when McIlroy connected with a Bingham cross to send the ball just wide of the post.

Almost immediately the visitors responded with a thrusting attack that ended with Da Costa crashing the ball into the side netting of Uprichard's goal. Italy looked dangerous on the break, turning defence quickly into attack, as when Ferrario cleared the ball to Schiaffino who combined with Montuori to leave Pivatelli with the chance to shoot but again it went wide, a feat he was to repeat on a number of occasions. Northern Ireland, however, always looked keener and sharper, with Blanchflower making good use of the space available to him while Bingham and Cush posed a constant threat down the right wing. Already it was turning into a classic end-to-end encounter.

With about fourteen minutes played, McParland beat Vincenzi on the left but then lost control of the ball. Peacock, however, was supporting his winger and regained possession for the home side, passing to McIlroy. Twenty-five yards from goal, McIlroy took the ball in his stride and unleashed a spectacular shot which sailed past the diving Bugatti. First blood to Northern Ireland.

Still reeling from this blow, the Italians almost conceded a second a few moments later. Again the danger came from the left where McParland was hacked down by Vincenzi. Peacock's free-kick found Simpson just six yards from the goal but his swivelling shot was somehow pushed up and over the bar by Bugatti.

For a period of about ten minutes the Italians were then in the ascendancy, seeking an equaliser, and Danny Blanchflower was forced to abandon his attacking role to support an increasingly hard pressed defence. One overhit back pass from McMichael had Northern Ireland fans' hearts in their mouths but Uprichard gathered the ball safely, one of a number of good stops he made at this vital stage, particularly from Da Costa.

Danny Blanchflower may have been doing more defending than attacking as the first half wore on, but it was his precision pass that put Wilbur Cush clear of the Italian defence in the twenty-ninth minute. Cush had time and space to strike a clean shot but Bugatti made a wonderful save, diving to his right. However, he could not hold the ball and Northern Ireland's diminutive inside-forward (playing in his fourth different position for his country) made no mistake from the follow-up. Windsor Park erupted. The home side were content to maintain their two-goal advantage to half-time.

The second half was largely a tale of Italy throwing everything they had at Doherty's team to get back in the game, Ghiggia and Montuori the main inspiration for the Azzuri. In football, a 2-0 advantage can very quickly be turned around, and Northern Ireland had Uprichard to thank for a string of fine saves, especially one to deny Pivatelli. Harry Gregg's stand-in was turning out to be one of the afternoon's heroes; until disaster struck in the ten minutes after half-time.

Ironically, Billy Simpson had gone close to making the score 3-0 five minutes earlier and McIlroy had glided past three opponents only to misplace his pass to Cush but now the Italians mounted an attack, Ghiggia feeding the ball to Montuori. Montuori's cross was of the type Uprichard had been handling comfortably all afternoon; this time he did not and the ball fell to the feet of the grateful Da Costa whose finish was only a formality. The fragility of a 2-0 lead was confirmed: Italy were back in the match and there were still thirty-five minutes left. Uprichard recalled his mistake later:

As the ball was coming down [from Montuori's cross], I changed my mind. First I was going to stretch up for the ball and then decided to let it drop into my arms. It had tremendous spin and as soon as it touched me it was away from my grasp. I tried to retrieve the ball, but it was too late and when Da Costa helped the ball on its way into the net my only wish was that the ground would open up and swallow me.[14]

Northern Ireland's performance now stuttered, almost a case of belated stagefright. A place in the World Cup finals had seemed secure; now their grasp was weakening. From Ghiggia's corner, Da Costa headed goalwards but the ball landed on top of the crossbar. It was pure agony for the Ulster supporters, encouraged though they were by the stalwart defending of Jackie Blanchflower. From a forward's perspective, McParland recalls that 'they went for us' but the back line were equal to the task: 'I thought our defence then under that pressure at the time was absolutely fantastic.' What had been a 'tense, hard battle … on a heavy pitch (Windsor was at its worst condition)' now became a war of nerves, skill and character. To his credit, Uprichard recovered well from the goal and, as he remembers, 'made a couple of good saves after that'.

Then Zsolt intervened. The man who had caused so much controversy by his absence on 4 December, took the limelight again, if only briefly. Determined that there would be no repeat of the 'battle' that Tommy Mitchell had presided over, the Hungarian referee had established his authority and imposed strict discipline from the first whistle. Now, however, he may have overcompensated for the slack refereeing in the December match. With Italy mounting yet another attack, this time down the right in the sixty-eighth minute, Alfie McMichael made a firm yet fair challenge on Ghiggia. The former Uruguayan World Cup winner reacted instinctively, trying to catch McMichael with his heel. The Northern Ireland left-back recalled afterwards: 'I kicked the ball clear and then found myself on the turf.'[17] It probably deserved a booking – Peter McParland thought it a 'nothing situation' – but Zsolt had no hesitation in ordering Ghiggia off the field. McMichael even appealed for leniency on Ghiggia's behalf but to no avail: 'I asked the referee to let Ghiggia stay on because I thought the sending off was harsh, but he waved me away.'[16] The Italians were down to ten men.

It was a blow from which they never recovered. Northern Ireland now seized control of the game and were unlucky not to win a penalty in the seventy-seventh minute when Jimmy McIlroy's cross appeared to be handled by Invernezzi. Six minutes later the ball was in the Italian net, but Simpson's effort was ruled out for offside, a debatable decision as Corradi appeared to be playing him on. In the dying minutes, McIlroy, who had been at his brilliant best all afternoon, again went close but nothing more was required. The final whistle in this Northern Ireland–Italy game heralded celebration, not confrontation.

Peter Doherty was naturally in an ebullient mood: 'Nobody gave us a chance of reaching Sweden. Now nobody will give us a chance of doing well there. But this team which has been together for four or five years is a happy family and has not yet reached its peak.'[17] For captain Danny Blanchflower, the key to the team's success had been its positive approach: 'We really deserved our victory and might have won easier. We were determined to keep attacking and it paid.'[18]

Although the *Northern Whig* speculated that 'the banks of the Tiber might well be over-flowing with tears'[19], the former world champions were gracious in defeat. The president of the Italian Football Federation acknowledged: 'The Irish played the more forthright football. Our lads played too much together in the first half and showed little signs of breaking through because of the stout Irish defence.'[20] It was an assessment seconded by the man who had masterminded Italy's triumphs in the World Cup in the 1930s, Vittorio Pozzo: 'With forwards who do not show vigour, determination, and ball control, we could not hope to pierce a tough defence – a wise, cautious and strong defence – such as that which Northern Ireland demonstrated.'[21]

It was a defence in which Jackie Blanchflower had been outstanding, possibly his best game as an international. But every man had played his part in a truly memorable victory, Jimmy McIlroy to the extent that he was even approached by Sampdoria about a move to Italian football. He reveals that the club offered him a villa overlooking the Mediterranean, arrangements for his children to attend an international school, and the chance to earn a lot more money than he would in Britain. But when he put the idea to his wife, a born-and-bred Lancashire girl, her response was, 'Why would you want to leave Burnley?' Quite.

In any event, Northern Ireland were on their way to Sweden ... or were they?

1. *Belfast News-Letter*, 2 December 1957.
2. Billy Bingham, *Soccer With the Stars*, The Soccer Book Club, London 1964, p. 107.
3. Ibid., p. 108.
4. Harry Gregg with Roger Anderson, *Harry's Game: The Autobiography*, Mainstream Publishing, Edinburgh, 2002, p. 85.
5. Danny Blanchflower, *The Double and Before ...*, Nicholas Kaye Limited, London, 1961, pp. 156–7.
6. *Irish News*, 5 December 1957.
7. *Belfast News-Letter*, 6 December 1957.
8. *Belfast Telegraph*, 9 December 1957.
9. *Belfast News-Letter*, 10 December 1957.
10. *Irish News*, 13 January 1958.
11. Ibid.
12. *Belfast Telegraph*, 13 January 1958.
13. *Northern Whig*, 16 January 1958.
14. *Belfast News-Letter*, 16 January 1958.

15. *Irish News*, 16 January 1958.
16. Ibid
17. Ibid.
18. Ibid.
19. *Northern Whig*, 16 January 1958.
20. Ibid.
21. *Belfast Telegraph*, 16 January 1958.

FIVE

NEVER ON A SUNDAY

The mood in the Northern Ireland dressing room after the Italy game should have been euphoric, and up to a point it was. The players were naturally elated at what they had achieved; nonetheless, there was a spectre at this feast, one that had been haunting the side for some months, for Northern Ireland might be prevented from taking part in the World Cup finals by the rules of their own governing body.

FIFA had set match dates for the final competition in Sweden which included a number of Sunday games but under IFA rules, football was not permitted on the Sabbath, either in Northern Ireland or in respect of the Northern Ireland team playing outside their own jurisdiction. Article 32, clause 2, stated that 'no match shall be played inside or outside this area [Northern Ireland] by this Association on a Sunday'.[1] It had been hoped that the AGM of the IFA back in May 1957 would relax the rule about playing Sunday football outside Northern Ireland but in fact the ban had been endorsed by an overwhelming majority of delegates (89-7). At that meeting, the Irish Churches League (with seventy-six affiliated clubs), headed by chairman John McMaster, stood resolutely opposed to any alteration to the rules but others had spoken up for change. Michael McColgan, supporting an alteration to Article 32, pointed out that in 1941 the four British associations had agreed in principle to the playing of Sunday football outside their respective jurisdictions, the resolution to be given effect by the adoption of a suitable article to their respective rules. The IFA was the only home association not to have done so.

It was generally believed that most Irish League clubs and senior officials in the IFA wanted the ban lifted but the voting power was held by those in favour of its retention: delegates from the junior and churches leagues, the grass roots of Northern Ireland football. Peter McParland also asserts that many in the IFA wanted the team to go to Sweden but lacked the courage of their convictions to speak out against the ban, preferring the option of 'sitting on the fence'. Beating Italy, therefore, was only half the battle to reach the World Cup finals.

As the players savoured success on 15 January 1958, Jimmy McIlroy asked IFA selector Jack Doherty, 'Is all this effort going to be wasted? Have we qualified for the World Cup simply to withdraw?' The response at least offered some hope: 'You boys have done your bit out there on the field. Now we'll carry on the fight in the legislation chamber.'[2] It was a 'fight' that could go either way.

Even on this day of victory, the essence of the argument as to whether or not Northern Ireland should compete in Sweden was captured in the statements of two of the IFA's most senior officers. Secretary Billy Drennan hinted at the need for compromise: 'We have a rule against playing on Sundays. That will have to be discussed before we go to Sweden.'[3] The emphasis here seemed to be on the IFA to move. However, for Sammy Walker, chairman of the selection committee and president of the Irish League, the onus was on FIFA to act. Indeed, Walker sounded quite blasé about the matter, expecting all the other competitors in the World Cup to accommodate Northern Ireland:

It may be taken for granted that the Association [IFA] will go forward to the final stages. There are mid-week dates and should we be drawn to play on a Sunday there is nothing to prevent the match from being arranged for another day.

> There is nothing in the rules of the World Cup to say that any or certain games must be played on a Sunday. It is known that the Irish FA have a complete ban on Sunday football, and I am sure our wishes will be respected by the other Associations.[4]

Walker's view was endorsed by IFA Vice-President William Wilton who stated that, 'Our articles prohibit us from playing matches on a Sunday and our wishes should be respected.'[5] Wilton had been stung into issuing this declaration by a report that the secretary of the Swedish FA had speculated that if Northern Ireland refused to play on Sunday then they may be replaced by Italy in the finals. Danny Blanchflower arguably took a more realistic view, telling BBC radio that he did not expect FIFA to change their rules and arrangements to suit the IFA but at the same time appreciated that the IFA had a duty to state their case in recognition of their rules.

In this increasingly secular age, it is not easy to capture the passion aroused by the issue of Sunday observance. Even in Northern Ireland in 2008 we are accustomed to going shopping or to the cinema seven days a week – in 1958 the 'never on a Sunday' rule was solidly in place. Northern Ireland's qualification therefore meant much soul searching and, on the part of those who were pro-ban, a quest for a solution that would not compromise their principles. Some, such as Sammy Walker, suggested petitioning FIFA to rearrange Northern Ireland's Sunday fixtures for a Saturday but this was simply not an option. There was a real fear, and prospect, that Northern Ireland might have to withdraw – inconceivable as it appears from our perspective – with all that might mean for the future of Northern Ireland international football, to say nothing of the £800 fine the IFA would have to pay FIFA (rising to £1,600 if withdrawal took place nearer the time of the finals).

Harry Gregg was one of those who was deeply troubled by the question of playing football on a Sunday – in fact, as he recalls it, no other player was as deeply affected by the question as himself. Peter McParland agrees with this assessment, pointing out that most of the team had played Sunday football before, during end-of-season tours with the clubs in Europe, and were somewhat nonplussed by the controversy. He also remembers that when team members encountered each other on club duty over the ensuing weeks, all were resolved to go to Sweden. McParland certainly was: he remembers travelling from Newry to a friend's house in Rathfriland, a twenty-four-mile round trip, just to watch the World Cup matches in Switzerland in 1954 because he could not get a TV reception at home – he was not prepared to now throw up the chance to play in the World Cup finals himself. 'It never entered our heads,' Billy Bingham adds, 'that Northern Ireland wouldn't be in Sweden. This was the climax of our career[s].'

Such determination was as yet not publicly stated but it came in the face of much heated debate on the topic and despite the pressure from certain religious groups such as the one that sent a letter to all the team members within a week of the Italy game, urging them not to play on Sunday. McParland cannot now recall with certainty who sent the letter, but the name Glass does stick in his mind and he wonders if the Revd Ian Paisley was involved in some way. Certainly Paisley did have an associate by the name of Jack Glass, though his ministry was in Glasgow. Nonetheless, whoever was responsible for mailing the Northern Ireland players, in this instance found their message and appeal went unheeded, with the possible exception of Harry Gregg.

Gregg had been brought up to observe the Sabbath as the Lord's Day and now agonised over the prospect of breaking God's Law. When Manchester United visited Blackpool, Gregg searched the telephone directory to find a clergyman from whom he could seek guidance on the matter. The minister he eventually spoke to posed the question whether Gregg thought it was all right for a surgeon to save the life of a child on a Sunday. It was a question that answered itself and crystallised the whole matter for the Northern Ireland 'keeper, seemingly providing the reassurance he needed. The counter-argument of course was that playing football was not a matter of life and death, irrespective of Bill Shankly's famous comment.

Harry Gregg's personal resolution, however, like that of any of the players, had no bearing on what the IFA would decide in relation to Sweden. Anti-ban forces were nonetheless encouraged by the outcome of a number of relevant meetings towards the end of January 1958. On Friday, 21 January, the Executive Committee of the Ulster Federation of Supporters' Clubs met in Belfast and announced their support for Northern Ireland playing in Sweden, even if it involved Sunday football. Delegates attending meetings of the Belfast Minor Football League and the Irish Alliance League voted in favour of lifting the Sunday ban for the duration of the World Cup in Sweden, and a similar position was adopted by the North East Referees Association. There was perhaps a prospect that votes were shifting but the seventy-five per cent majority needed to change the IFA Sunday rule was still a formidable hurdle.

On 25 January a meeting of Irish League Management Committee and IFA divisional representatives passed a recommendation that the Northern Ireland team be sent to Sweden 'without conditions' – whatever that meant. The proposal was considered by a meeting of the IFA International Committee later the same day but no public announcement was made. The expectation was that the proposal – to go to Sweden – would be put before the IFA Council at its monthly meeting, scheduled for 28 January.

The day before the IFA Council convened, representatives of the Amateur League gathered in Clarence Place Hall in

Belfast to debate the issue. Here, no clear consensus emerged but rather a repetition of the familiar arguments. Those in favour of lifting the ban made the point that the IFA had always been aware of the inevitability of Sunday games in the final competition and therefore must honour the commitment that was implicit in entering the qualifying phase: to send a team to the finals in Sweden. If the Association had had concerns about the issue, then it should have withdrawn from the competition in May 1957 when the AGM had voted against amending Article 32. Opposing voices argued that it was perfectly reasonable to ask FIFA to accommodate the religious principles in question, failing to accept that it was rather late in the day to make such a case. These opponents of change received support on the same night from a meeting of the Belfast District Synod of the Methodist Church which publicly urged the IFA not to compromise on the Sunday football question.

The decision of the IFA Council on 28 January was to both play and appeal. By twenty votes to eight (and one abstention), delegates approved Northern Ireland competing in Sweden but at the same time the IFA was also to forward a request to the FIFA Organising Committee (due to meet on 8 February) to have the Sunday games rearranged. If FIFA said no (as everyone expected) then the Northern Ireland team would play on the designated dates.

As a gesture to the Sunday ban supporters, players were to be allowed to make their own individual decision about playing on a Sunday, though no withdrawals were anticipated. The IFA declared that 'no player should be required to play on a Sunday if he objects to do so'[6] and that 'no player should be omitted from the party for this reason'.[7] Carefully sidestepping the possibility of a rebellion from below (by those in favour of the Sunday ban), the Council also rejected by twenty votes to nine a proposal to bring the issue to an extraordinary general meeting of the IFA.

The draw for the World Cup finals groups was held on 8 February when the FIFA Organising Committee also confirmed that no fixture dates would be changed. According to Swedish officials attending the draw in Stockholm, the IFA request was not even considered by FIFA, their attitude being that in entering the qualifying competition, the IFA had tacitly accepted FIFA rules. In a seeded draw in which each group was to contain one team from the United Kingdom, one from Western Europe, one from behind the Iron Curtain, and one from Central/South America, Northern Ireland found themselves in the same group as Czechoslovakia, Argentina and reigning world champions West Germany. Their first game, against the Czechs, was scheduled for a Sunday (8 June), as was their last group match on 15 June.

If the IFA thought that the matter was settled, they were being supremely optimistic. Just two days after FIFA had announced the group fixtures for Sweden, the Methodist Council on Social Welfare issued a resolution in which it appealed to the Council of the IFA to 'abide by the spirit of its own rules and to advise members of the Irish team not to play on Sundays'.[8] Certainly, the Churches League did not consider the fight over, or lost. Meeting in the City YMCA on Thursday, 13 February, it was proposed to call for an extraordinary general meeting of the IFA to discuss the Sunday ban, which in the Churches League's opinion still stood and therefore still denied the IFA the right to take a Northern Ireland team to the World Cup. Should the IFA refuse an extraordinary general meeting, then the Churches League was ready to seek an injunction preventing the Irish Football Association giving effect to its own resolution to compete in the World Cup finals.

In retrospect, the climax of the protest campaign against the international team being prepared to play on a Sunday came on 16 February (a Sunday, by the way), when a meeting was convened in the Assembly Hall in Belfast of many of the public representatives opposed to Sunday football. All the main Protestant denominations were represented and the meeting was presided over by the Very Reverend Dr AF Moody, former moderator of the Presbyterian Church. The platform party also included the vice-president of the IFA, William Wilton (perhaps, appropriately, an undertaker by profession).

The IFA was accused of hypocrisy in that their rules not only prohibited players and clubs playing on Sunday but even outlawed the signing of a player by a club on a Sunday. Canon Maguire, of the Church of Ireland, argued that if Sunday football was accepted then there would be demands for cinema and concerts on Sunday, and that the Lord's Day would change out of all recognition – which of course it has. (Belfast City Council may have taken heed of this warning, as some weeks later they voted against permitting band concerts on Sunday in their parks in the coming summer.) The fundamental point, however, as expressed by the Revd Rupert Gibson of the Presbyterian Church, was that the IFA was not just in breach of their own articles of association but the Law of God.

The Revd Hubert Irvine, a Methodist minister from Dunmurry, made a more ominous contribution: 'I inform and warn the IFA Council here and now that everything possible will be done to force them if need be to abide by the Articles of Association which forbids [sic] Sunday football inside or outside the area of their jurisdiction.'[9] The 'everything possible' that Revd Irvine referred to apparently included legal action to stop Northern Ireland playing in the World Cup finals if it meant playing on a Sunday. This was not a threat the IFA could afford to ignore.

Four days after the protest meeting, the IFA Emergency Committee convened to consider a formal letter from the Churches League asking the IFA to reverse its decision to allow the international team to play in Sweden. In keeping with the mood set by Revd Irvine in his public statement, the letter also threatened 'further necessary steps'[10] if a satisfactory response was not received. Although the committee reaffirmed the decision to compete in the World Cup finals, moves were also initiated to try to reach a diplomatic solution to the impasse.

On 13 March the IFA met with representatives of the Churches League to try to resolve the dispute: the outcome was an agreement by the Churches to withdraw their opposition to the international side playing on Sunday in Sweden in return for an IFA commitment not to enter a team in any future competition that would involve Sunday football. The football authorities knew that they would have to pay a price for the chance to compete in Sweden but this appeared to be quite a high one. The problem in question had been shelved rather than resolved; it was a fudge rather than a final settlement.

The joint statement issued by the IFA and the Churches League declared that 'no team under its [the IFA's] jurisdiction shall again enter or be permitted to enter for any competition, or play in any international matches, in which the team would be required to play on a Sunday'.[11] As if to prove that these were not mere words, the IFA Emergency Committee instructed IFA Secretary Billy Drennan to withdraw the Northern Ireland youth team from a European tournament to be played in Luxembourg at the beginning of April because the organisers could not guarantee that the team would not have to play on a Sunday. It may have been largely a gesture to those who were still unhappy about the senior side competing in Sweden, but it was an important gesture nonetheless.

At last, almost exactly two months after the 2-1 defeat of Italy, and with less than three months to their opening game against Czechoslovakia, Northern Ireland were on their way to the World Cup finals. As a postscript to this amazing saga, the Northern Ireland selector who accompanied Harry Gregg on his train and boat journey to the competition (Gregg not flying with his colleagues because of his involvement in the Munich air disaster) – Joe Beckett – immediately returned home as he refused to attend a tournament in which the team played on a Sunday. They say that sport and politics don't mix but sport and religion is clearly an equally volatile combination.

Meanwhile, what about the team and the players I hear you ask? Well, football was still being played (though not on a Sunday) and events both dramatic and tragic were unfolding. On 20 January, just five days after the win over Italy, Peter Doherty handed in his resignation as manager of Doncaster Rovers, the team he had served since May 1949, first as player-manager, guiding them from the Third Division (North) to the Second Division. Just over a week later, he was appointed manager of Bristol City (proving that in 1958 you could believe at least some of the things you read in the papers).

Doherty's move was probably good news for him, after a recent unhappy spell at Doncaster, but the events of which he learned on 6 and 7 February were definitely not. In purely football terms the Munich air crash was a disaster for Manchester United and England, but also for Northern Ireland. Harry Gregg had emerged relatively unscathed but as we know Jackie Blanchflower had not been so lucky. The twenty-four-year-old centre-half would remain in hospital until 13 March (coincidentally the day of the agreement between the IFA and Churches League) and would, in fact, never again play top-class football. Aside from the personal tragedy, which quite naturally and correctly dominated the public and press response to the event, Northern Ireland had no ready-made replacement. It was a severe blow to Doherty's plans and the team's hopes.

Between qualifying for the World Cup and their opening match in the tournament, Northern Ireland played only one game: their final British Championship outing of the 1957–58 season, against Wales at Ninian Park, Cardiff, on 16 April. If Northern Ireland won this game then they would be British champions for the first time since 1914 (their only previous success).

Wales, like Northern Ireland, were also preparing for Sweden, though their qualification had been much more fortuitous. Having finished second in their qualifying group (to Czechoslovakia), Wales earned a reprieve due to the collapse of the Afro–Asia qualifying group. When Egypt, Sudan and Indonesia withdrew from the competition, Israel were left with no opposition and FIFA decreed that the names of all the runners-up in the other qualifying groups be put in a draw to face the Israelis. Wales won the lottery and went on to defeat Israel by 2-0 in both legs of the eliminator.

Doherty was now forced to address the problem of the loss of Jackie Blanchflower. His response was to draft in Dick Keith, normally a right-back, at centre-half, with the right-back position going to Willie Cunningham. The rest of the team was as expected:

N Ireland: Gregg (Manchester Utd); Cunningham (Leicester City), McMichael (Newcastle Utd); Blanchflower (Tottenham Hotspur), Keith (Newcastle Utd), Peacock (Celtic); Bingham (Sunderland), Cush (Leeds Utd), Simpson (Rangers), McIlroy (Burnley), McParland (Aston Villa).

It was not one of Northern Ireland's better performances, lacking co-ordination and fluency, yet they appeared to have the game in their grip when Cush, evading both Welsh left-half Brown and left-back Hopkins, broke down the right and crossed for Simpson to head home in the sixty-fifth minute. Welsh appeals for offside were turned away and the British Championship appeared to be Windsor-bound. The 1-0 lead was held until four minutes from the end when a speculative

Stairway to heaven? The Northern Ireland squad for Sweden (minus Keith, McMichael and Gregg who were travelling independently of the main party). Standing on the left of the stairway, from the top down, are Derek Dougan, Billy Bingham, Gerry Morgan (trainer), Willie Cunningham, Peter McParland, Sammy McCrory, Wilbur Cush, Danny Blanchflower and (on the ground) Bertie Peacock. On the right of the stairway, again from the top, are Norman Uprichard, Fay Coyle, Jimmy McIlroy, Jackie Scott, Tommy Casey, Billy Simpson and (on the ground) Peter Doherty (manager). (*Belfast Telegraph*)

Billy Bingham in his Sunderland shirt.

(top) The headquarters at Tylösand.
(bottom) Wilbur Cush talks to Jack Doherty of the IFA while
Danny Blanchflower and Peter Doherty discuss tactics in the background
(*Belfast Telegraph*)

(top) left: Wilbur Cush; right: Norman Uprichard
(bottom) left: Alf McMichael; right: Derek Dougan

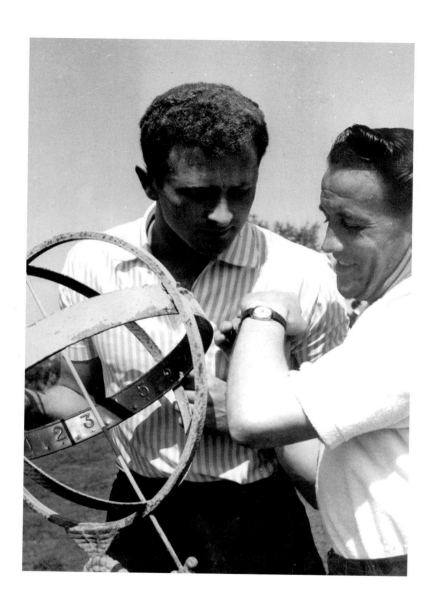

Harry Gregg goes for an exotic timepiece while Wilbur Cush prefers
something more modern. (*Belfast Telegraph*)

Billy Bingham 'does a Ronaldo' between the legs of fellow-winger Peter McParland during training in Sweden.(*Belfast Telegraph*).

Jimmy McIlroy is 'on the ball', literally, as he practises his throw-in. The player lacing up his boots in the background is Danny Blanchflower. (*Belfast Telegraph*).

(top) Billy Simpson watches as Wilbur Cush risks a hamstring strain during the pre-World Cup training at Windsor Park. (bottom) Bertie Peacock (centre) has obviously resigned himself to not getting a word in with captain Danny Blanchflower (left) and manager Peter Doherty before Northern Ireland's opening group match against Czechoslovakia. (*Belfast Telegraph*)

shot from the Welsh inside-forward Ron Hewitt took a deflection off Keith and ran past Harry Gregg who was, in the words of the *Belfast Telegraph*, 'standing like a statue'.

The result was disappointing (Northern Ireland eventually sharing the British Championship with England who defeated Scotland 4-0 at Hampden Park) but so too was the way the team had played. The *Belfast Telegraph* correspondent Malcolm Brodie was particularly critical of Peter McParland, remarking that he had as many chances to score as 'France has had post-war Governments'. Brodie's unequivocal conclusion was that the Villa outside-left should be dropped from the team: 'With the exception of his first international at Wrexham a few years ago he has never shown a glimpse of the form which has made him one of his club's leading powers. Last night he wrote his obituary.' Brodie's assessment was very much in tone with the *Belfast News-Letter*'s verdict after the Italy match in January when it had speculated that the international selectors 'may think twice before calling on him [McParland] again'.

McParland dismisses the Brodie attack as nothing out of the ordinary: 'He had a go [at some time] at most of the players, most of the players anyway ... I don't know if he said anything [derogatory] about Harry [Gregg] because Harry would have given him a punch.' He does, however, acknowledge that he had a poor game against Wales, to the point where he speculated with Willie Cunningham that he might not make the squad for Sweden. If he was seeking reassurance from his team-mate, it came in a distinctly backhanded fashion: 'What do you mean [about not making the squad] – we've only got sixteen players!' A fair point – if made with a degree of insensitivity – but in any event, Peter McParland's reply to Malcolm Brodie and the other doubters would come in June, and on the field.

One of those watching the Wales match with special interest was the West German manager Sepp Herberger, whose side would face Northern Ireland in the qualifying group. He was quite happy with what he saw, though his after-match comment did have a note of caution: 'I have no worries but I think Ireland cannot play as badly again.'[12]

Quite possibly a few more friendly games might have allowed the team to iron out the problems that had manifested themselves at Ninian Park, especially in the goalscoring department, and Northern Ireland did receive invites from Denmark, France and even Juventus. However, the IFA felt obliged to turn down all such approaches as they could not afford the risk of having players injured, apart from the fact that it was always difficult getting players released by their clubs. As for the luxury of dropping a leading First Division forward like Peter McParland, as Malcolm Brodie suggested, it just wasn't going to happen.

On 29 April, the IFA announced a squad of sixteen players for Sweden. The permitted number was twenty-two but such were the limited resources available to Northern Ireland that a number of places went unfilled. (The earlier FIFA request for a preliminary squad of forty players was treated with incredulity at IFA headquarters.) A late addition to the list was Fay Coyle of Nottingham Forest (transferred to the English club from Coleraine just a few weeks earlier), bringing the final squad number up to seventeen. The quad was:

Goalkeepers: Gregg (Manchester Utd), Uprichard (Portsmouth). Full-backs: Cunningham (Leicester City), Keith (Newcastle Utd), McMichael (Newcastle Utd). Half-backs: Blanchflower (Tottenham Hotspur), Casey (Newcastle Utd), Peacock (Celtic). Forwards: Bingham (Sunderland), Coyle (Nottingham Forest), Cush (Leeds Utd), Dougan (Portsmouth), McCrory (Southend Utd), McIlroy (Burnley), McParland (Aston Villa), Scott (Grimsby Town), Simpson (Rangers).

A further five players were registered with FIFA (to make up the complement of twenty-two places) but they would only travel to Sweden if other players had to drop out through injury or for any other reason. The five stand-bys were Sammy Chapman (Portsmouth), Len Grahan (Doncaster Rovers), Tommy Hamill (Linfield), Roy Rea (Glenavon) and Robin Trainor (Coleraine).

Northern Ireland may have been lacking in terms of quantity but, despite the recent showing against Wales, the quality of the team was never really in question. It even included the player recently named Footballer of the Year by England's football writers: Danny Blanchflower of Spurs. One observer who rated the Northern Ireland captain, and his team, highly was the man who had officiated at the final qualifying match at Windsor Park in January. Istvan Zsolt told the Hungarian news agency *MTI*:

> The national team of Northern Ireland is a team of players in excellent condition who play with great stamina for the whole of the ninety minutes ... Their players are well trained, can use both feet equally well ... On the basis of their match against Italy, they are almost as good a team as the Soviet and West German sides. Their best players were J. Blanchflower centre-half, D. Blanchflower, right-half, and the right-winger Bingham.[13]

It was Danny Blanchflower who initially took charge of the squad that began to assemble at Windsor Park on Monday, 12 May, just a month away from Northern Ireland's opening game in Sweden. Peter Doherty was currently on tour with his club side, Bristol City, and amazingly most of the squad were also so engaged. In our modern game, burdened down as it is with competitions, it is inconceivable that a club tour should be given such a high priority. A club tour in 1958, however, conjured up visions of exotic foreign locations and a reward for the hard slog of the English football season. In fact only six of the Northern Ireland squad were free of club commitments and able to report for duty that particular Monday: Blanchflower, Uprichard, Dougan, Casey, Bingham and Cush. The others were on club tours, apart from Harry Gregg who was due to appear for Manchester United in the second leg of the European Cup semi-final against AC Milan in Milan on Wednesday (United lost 4-0 to go out 4-1 on aggregate).

The plan was for the squad (or what there was of it) to spend two weeks in Belfast before leaving for London where they would be joined by Doherty. In Belfast the players worked hard under Blanchflower to reach the peak of physical condition, the daily routine usually incorporating long road runs in the upper Lagan valley, half-lap sprints around Windsor Park, and press-ups, before concluding with a five-a-side match. Peter McParland looks back with a smile – he was still on club duty with Aston Villa – as he remembers what the Belfast contingent had to endure, remarking that Danny 'knocked their pan in', though it did leave the players 'nicely tuned up' when they got to Sweden, thereafter only needing light work such as sprinting and technical sessions.

The Northern Ireland captain had once criticised the over-emphasis on physical preparation in English club football, but he was no easy taskmaster himself when given responsibility. Nonetheless the spirit was good, and, as Peter McParland suggests, the flesh was not in bad shape either.

The Newcastle full-back pair Dick Keith and Alfie McMichael were due to join the squad in London after returning from their club's tour of Romania but a number of delays threw the Newcastle itinerary into confusion, and the players missed the London rendezvous. In fact Keith and McMichael ended up flying direct to Gothenburg to join the Northern Ireland party in Sweden.

The official party flew from London to Copenhagen on 2 June and then travelled to Malmö by ferry. The players then faced an arduous coach journey to their camp in Tylösand, on the 'Swedish Riviera', but this was circumvented by taking another ferry, this time from Halsingor to Halsingborg. Foreign travel really was an adventure in 1958.

This applied even more so in the case of Harry Gregg. The IFA had decided that after his experiences at Munich the Manchester United 'keeper should travel to Copenhagen by train and boat, accompanied by Beckett. This meant that the agonising decision of whether or not to fly was taken out of Gregg's hands, allowing the player to concentrate on his football. In fact the IFA selectors had been closely monitoring the 'keeper's performances post-Munich to confirm that he was up to the rigours of the World Cup. They felt he was – and how right they were.

Located just six miles west of Halmstad where they were due to play two of their group matches, Tylösand, on Sweden's west coast and its leading summer resort, was to be Northern Ireland's 'home' for the next few weeks. IFA Secretary Billy Drennan, aware that the Czechs also had their eyes on Tylösand, had flown direct from the World Cup draw in Stockholm in February to Malmö to keep ahead of his European rivals. Although Drennan's plane was delayed from taking off for four hours due to bad weather, Czech officials fared much worse on the roads, their car at one point getting stuck in a snowdrift. Drennan won the race to Tylösand with two hours to spare and the coveted location was secured for the Ulstermen.

The resort had a number of hotels and the team, officials, and press each stayed in a different hotel but always dined together, usually at the team venue which was managed by Haken Wallberg. Norman Uprichard remembers the accommodation as chalet-style and much to his liking.

Tylösand was a choice that quickly won the approval of the players, Jimmy McIlroy summing up: 'The Irish team could not have chosen a better spot for their headquarters. Just a collection of chalets and beach huts and a luxury hotel overlooking a sandy beach.'[14] (Today Tylösand is dominated by the ultra-modern Nya Hotel Tylösand complex.) One theory as to why Northern Ireland did so well in the competition – and one to which McIlroy would have subscribed – was that the players were able to completely relax in this quiet resort and also enjoy looking at the beautiful Swedish girls on Tylösand beach!

Certainly, the Northern Ireland build-up to their opening game appeared almost casual, the daily routine usually one of training in the morning; beach in the afternoon; cards, letter-writing or golf in the evening. How much this routine was due to the ambience, the fact that Northern Ireland were underdogs in the competition, or the usual approach of Peter Doherty, is difficult to gauge. Without doubt, Northern Ireland fell in love with Tylösand and the local Swedes reciprocated by adopting the Ulstermen as 'their team'. The players frequented the shops in the area and even attended the local church, becoming well known and well liked.

One young Swedish boy in particular became very attached to the visitors. Thirteen-year-old Bengt Jonasson was captivated by the excitement of his home town hosting one of the World Cup competitors and could not keep himself away from the Northern Ireland camp. At first the only Northern Ireland player he knew was Harry Gregg, whose heroism in Munich had preceded him, and when the team coach arrived at the hotel, the young blond-haired Bengt approached the famous 'keeper with a piece of paper and a request: 'Meester Gregg, could you sign for me?'[15]

Bengt, in a way, became the team's unofficial mascot. He attended training sessions, travelled on the team bus to matches (including the 250-mile trip to Norrköping), sat on the bench at matches, attended civic receptions and even acted as an interpreter for players and officials on occasion. Most of all he enjoyed the antics of trainer Gerry Morgan and his 'Sergeant Bilko' shout. He was present at the team's farewell banquet (where he linked hands with Danny Blanchflower and Harry Gregg to sing 'Auld Lang Syne') and as a postscript was the special guest at the Northern Ireland–England game at Windsor Park in October, an idea originally suggested by Malcolm Brodie to Harry Gregg. The fact that the cost of Bengt's trip to Belfast was met by players, officials and reporters spoke volumes for the special relationship forged between Northern Ireland and Tylösand. As Wilbur Cush remarked at the time, 'This is really something. Just like playing at home.'[16]

That first 'home' game was against Czechoslovakia, the side Northern Ireland had beaten in the race to secure Tylösand as a team base. Could they win this one as well?

1. *Belfast News-Letter*, 17 February 1958.
2. Jimmy McIlroy, *Right Inside Soccer*, The Sportsman's Book Club, London, 1961, p. 27.
3. *Irish News*, 16 January 1958.
4. *Belfast News-Letter*, 16 January 1958.
5. Ibid., 17 January 1958.
6. *Belfast News-Letter*, 29 January 1958.
7. Ibid.
8. *Belfast Telegraph*, 10 February 1958.
9. *Irish News*, 17 February 1958.
10. Ibid., 26 February 1958.
11. *Belfast Telegraph*, 14 March 1958.
12. Ibid.
13. *Irish News*, 25 January 1958.
14. McIlroy, p. 29.
15. N Ireland v. England, Windsor Park, Belfast, 4 October 1958, official match programme.
16. Ibid.

SIX

BOUNCING THE CZECHS

After arriving in Sweden, Peter Doherty's first priority was to determine which eleven players would face Czechoslovakia in Northern Ireland's opening game. With such a small squad of players to choose from, this might have been considered a relatively straightforward task but a number of issues emerged to complicate matters.

Doherty's first-choice 'keeper was Harry Gregg, despite the recent trauma he had come through with Manchester United. However, the Munich disaster had left Gregg with sleep problems and it was decided that he should share a room with trainer Gerry Morgan. Just how the company of the ebullient Morgan was supposed to help Gregg overcome his insomnia I am not sure – it was a possible calculation that Gerry's antics would simply leave Harry exhausted by the end of the evening – but if Gregg's performances in the tournament are any indication, then it was undoubtedly effective therapy. Certainly there was always a laugh to be had, such as Gerry's frantic and frequent searches for his glasses, only for his room-mate to point out that they were perched on the trainer's head. As Gregg comments, 'If I wasn't mad beforehand, I was mad afterwards.'

Two other room-mates, as they had been for years, were Danny Blanchflower and Jimmy McIlroy, with Danny inevitably doing most of the talking, often late into the night. Conversation and subject matter tended to be eclectic, as McIlroy reminisces:

> ... he told me when he was at Aston Villa he'd maybe go into a café or a restaurant and just sit and watch people coming in and out [to try to] imagine what sort of person that would be. We kidded him that all he was there for was looking for the ladies ... but he maintained that he was studying human nature. I learnt a lot from Danny in every way – about life and about football.

There is also a footnote to the Blanchflower–McIlroy room-sharing arrangement that is worth mentioning. Jimmy recalls going to Manchester some years later to record a tribute for Danny's *This Is Your Life* appearance – which of course Blanchflower famously aborted – and the Burnley forward was asked how well he knew the Tottenham and Northern Ireland captain. He replied, 'I've known Danny for years, I've slept with him for years,' at which point the interview was cut and the producer suggested that McIlroy use the word 'roomed' instead of 'slept'. McIlroy and Blanchflower were certainly close but, as they say, not that close.

Back to Sweden, and an unforeseen worry for Northern Ireland was the late, late arrival of the Newcastle United full-backs Dick Keith and Alfie McMichael from their club tour. They had still not appeared by 3 June and Northern Ireland selector Harry Cavan had admitted to Malcolm Brodie that officials had 'no idea when we can expect them'.[1] This was hardly conducive to smooth preparations for the big game on 8 June. Keith and McMichael duly arrived on the Wednesday night, giving them just three full days to settle into the rhythm of the build-up to the Czech encounter, a far cry from today's meticulous approach by sides competing in the finals of the World Cup.

The question mark over the position of the centre-half had been troubling manager Doherty since the Munich crash. In the game against Wales, Dick Keith had been moved from right-back to the centre of the defence and had performed competently enough but an encounter with one of Europe's top sides was another matter. Wilbur Cush had, of course, demonstrated in the qualifying match against Italy in Rome that he could stand in for Jackie Blanchflower but he was much more effective at wing-half or inside-forward and Doherty did not want to deprive the midfield of the Lurgan man's powerhouse style.

As far as the manager was concerned, that left one option – to move the Leicester City right-back Willie Cunningham to the number five position. Cunningham had never played centre-half for club or country but he was an experienced defender who Doherty believed could adapt. It may have been something of a risk but it was a calculated one.

However, the Cunningham solution almost crashed before it had got off the ground when the player was found to be running a temperature on 3 June and was sent back to bed. Fortunately his recovery was quick.

The same could not be said for Billy Simpson who on the same day strained a thigh muscle during training. The chances of recovery in time for the match five days later were not good and Doherty's worst fears were confirmed when Simpson failed a strenuous fitness test on the Saturday, 7 June. Worse still, Simpson's injury would rule him out of not just the game against Czechoslovakia but the entire tournament.

Already missing their regular centre-half, Northern Ireland had now lost their first-choice centre-forward. Harry Gregg speculates that if Peter Doherty had been registered as a player for this tournament he would have been the best possible replacement for Simpson – the Northern Ireland manager celebrated his forty-fifth birthday on 6 June, and considering that Stanley Matthews was forty-two when he played his last game for England (in May 1957), the idea is maybe not as fanciful as it first appears. However, Doherty was not registered to play so the option was not available.

The question now was who would replace the Rangers striker, the contenders being Fay Coyle of Nottingham Forest and Dougan of Portsmouth, experience and youth personified respectively. Doherty went for youth. Dougan had not yet appeared for the senior team but had turned out earlier in the season for the Northern Ireland B side, scoring three of the team's six goals. A repeat showing was unlikely but Peter Doherty knew potential when he saw it and so 'the Doog' lined up for his first cap.

According to Harry Gregg, Dougan, perhaps because of his youth, was one of the easiest players to 'wind up' in the squad – along with Billy Bingham, or 'Bingy' as Gregg referred to him (and which Bingham apparently did not like). Gregg recalls Bingham being a bit full of himself, as someone, in Gregg's words, who 'lived on cloud seven' – which was presumably not as bad as cloud nine, or was perhaps the Irish equivalent. Bingham used to talk about his 'shares and investments' or his 'grand piano', producing nudges and winks from his colleagues as Gregg remembers. 'What's he on about' was the standard reaction, while the Sunderland player's affected accent still makes Gregg smile – 'a conceited little pup – but in a nice way'. Of course, what one person might consider an affected accent, another might find perfectly normal, though the chances are that the other person would not come from Ulster. Equally, for someone to find talking about stocks and shares or playing a grand piano somewhat pretentious suggests what we might call inverted snobbery. Such is the way of team sport, throwing together, as it does, those who can be as different as day and night. As for Bingham's reaction to Gregg, he acknowledges that he 'got on okay ... but he wasn't a bosom pal ... I wasn't his biggest mate'.

Ironically, Bingham's 'mate' at the World Cup, or at least the person he shared a room with, was the aforementioned Dougan. Though they had common roots in east Belfast –

'He had that affinity to me [sic] through that,' says Bingham – they did make an odd pair, 'the long and the short' as Bingham remembers being called. According to Bingham, Dougan 'was a bit temperamental' and 'didn't like anyone who was a bit toffee-nosed' but went out of his way to tag along with Bingham, who clearly still has a lot of affection for his old room-mate:

> He selected it [the rooming arrangement] more than me, so I went along with it. He was a rebel, sometimes I think, without a cause. He was always arguing about things, saying [this] was the wrong thing to do, [that] we should do [this instead] – always contentious. But he was quite funny, too.

In any event, the banter in the Northern Ireland camp was not just one-way, and overall the spirit was high, helping to take minds off those selection problems, if only for a time.

Aside from injuries, there was another concern that very much occupied Peter Doherty and his side: the quality of their opponents in the opening match. Czechoslovakia were one of the best teams in Europe, and had won Group Four in the European qualifying phase of the tournament, ahead of Wales and East Germany. Some commentators even fancied the Czechs to make it all the way to the final, if not to become champions.

It was Danny Blanchflower who suggested a trip to watch the Czechs play a warm-up match before the finals got underway. Doherty needed no convincing and selector Harry Cavan and *Belfast Telegraph* reporter Malcolm Brodie also decided to join the spying assignment.

It was not quite mission impossible but the journey to Copenhagen, where the Czechs were to play a Danish XI playing under the name of Alliancen, was still a formidable undertaking. Travelling in the car of their Swedish FA liaison man Frank Pearson, and reaching Denmark by ferry, it was a four-hour, one hundred-mile excursion.

The Czechs, managed by Karel Kolsky, manager of army side Dukla Prague, ran out comfortable 3-0 winners, impressing Danny Blanchflower with their style. He was mindful too of what Jimmy McIlroy had said about the high standard of Czech football, Burnley having recently toured the central European state and lost all their matches. Peter Doherty, however, was not intimidated by what he saw in Copenhagen. He believed the Czechs were beatable, telling the *Belfast Telegraph*:

> Their distribution is marvellous and they can control the ball with any part of their bodies. Their passes are quick and simple and the inside-forward pair can be devastating, but the entire team – all big-built – show signs of being easily rattled.[2]

Had Doherty identified the Czechs' Achilles heel? Could Northern Ireland knock them off their rhythm and seize the initiative? The Northern Ireland manager believed so. The Czech game was based on a fluent style but if that fluency could be disrupted by harrying and chasing then the threat might be neutralised. Doherty had faith in his own players and he made them believe in themselves, a belief that was reinforced by recall of the recent victory over Italy.

Doherty's planning was meticulous: this was not just a case of hustling the opposition into mistakes but of carefully moulding his playing resources to the task in hand. The first priority was to keep his team unit tight; therefore the wingers, Bingham and McParland, were to lie deep and left-half Peacock was to play a more defensive game than usual. This defensive foundation, however, was ultimately to be the springboard for attacks launched from the middle of the field by Blanchflower and McIlroy, while up front Dougan and Cush were to form a double spearhead to thrust at the Czech goal. When the Czechs themselves were driving at the Northern Ireland goal, the plan was to fall back to the penalty area and then challenge, but if the basic strategy worked – inhibiting the central Europeans' passing game – then a rearguard action would not be called for.

Halmstad, a small industrial port on the River Nissan with a population of around 40,000, was the seat of the provincial governor (in the seventeenth-century castle built by Christian IV of Denmark) and home to a Swedish first division club whose ground – the Orjans Voll stadium, built in 1922 but redeveloped for the World Cup – had a picturesque riverside setting. Into these almost idyllic surroundings the two teams stepped on Sunday, 8 June 1958.

In fact one of Peter McParland's most vivid memories of that opening game is of the arrival of the teams at the stadium. While the Northern Ireland bus, arriving just ahead of that of their opponents, was rocking to the strains of 'When Irish Eyes Are Smiling', as was their normal routine, the Czech bus had all its curtains drawn, presumably to protect Communist sensitivities from the decadence of the West – or to put it another way, to prevent the eastern Europeans from seeing the prosperity and freedom of the non-Communist world. It perhaps gave the Northern Ireland players a psychological boost to see the Czechs so closeted and cosseted, though whether that connoted a significant advantage remained to be seen.

The 10,647 shirt-sleeved crowd that greeted the teams included a number of die-hard supporters who had made the arduous journey from Northern Ireland. They included a Mr and Mrs Jim Morton from Stirling Gardens in Cregagh, Belfast; Jimmy McMullen of Grand Parade, Belfast; Leslie Nicholl from Newry; David McGrotty, Frankie Harte and

Mick McColgan from Coleraine, the latter an old school pal of Peter Doherty; former Coleraine player Stanley Mahood; and Billy Malcolmson who later was to assist Northern Ireland trainer Gerry Morgan treat the injured players as the casualty list built up in the course of the tournament. Also present were the Lord Mayor of Belfast, Alderman Cecil McKee, and his secretary David Newburn. In all, it was a small contingent from home but an extremely vocal one.

Another participant of note on this occasion was one of the linesmen – Arthur Ellis, the future referee on *It's a Knockout*. Ellis, of course, had very nearly been the referee for the Northern Ireland v Italy qualifying match the previous December (which turned out not to be a qualifying match) but now had a role to play in the latest act in this World Cup drama.

The team line-ups for this first game for Northern Ireland in a World Cup finals competition, and also their first ever on a Sunday, were as follows:

Northern Ireland: Gregg (Manchester Utd); Keith (Newcastle Utd), McMichael (Newcastle Utd); Blanchflower (Tottenham Hotspur), Cunningham (Leicester City), Peacock (Celtic); Bingham (Sunderland), Cush (Leeds Utd), Dougan (Portsmouth), McIlroy (Burnley), McParland (Aston Villa).
Czechoslovakia: Dolejsi; Mraz, Novak; Pluskal, Cadek, Masopust; Hovorka, Dvorak, Borovicka, Hertl, Kraus.

The game opened at a frantic pace with the first attack materialising down the Czech right, through Vaclav Hovorka, who won an early corner – indeed the Northern Ireland full-backs had their work cut out to contain both Czech wingers – but Danny Blanchflower soon took matters in hand to restore some calm, stroking a number of long through balls to new boy Dougan. Cush also began to assert himself in the middle of the field and in partnership with Bingham on the right wing. However, Northern Ireland's normal free-flowing, attacking game was not given full rein because of their commitment to dislocating the smooth running and passing of their opponents, no player rising to the challenge better than Bertie Peacock.

The Celtic player certainly caught the eye of the *Belfast Telegraph*'s correspondent, Malcolm Brodie: 'His tackling was fierce and fair, his pace the acme of accuracy and his general distribution left nothing to be desired. A five-star performance without any flaws and one which has made him the talk of Halmstad ...'[3] It was the Celtic player's distribution that particularly impressed team-mate Billy Bingham. 'Bertie was great at transferring the ball over to the right side,' informs Bingham. 'He could change the play, just dramatically like that,' Bingham snapping his fingers, 'and that changes the point of attack. The other team then has to move round to accommodate that. If they don't run round quick enough, then you were away – you were in business.'

Peacock looked comfortable in his assigned role from the very start but the same could not be said for all his colleagues. Recent rain had left the surface slippery and many of the Northern Ireland players found it difficult enough to keep their feet let alone tackle the opposition. It was not a very auspicious opening, further emphasised by the fact that the first serious threat on goal came from the Czechs with an attack down the left resulting in a testing cross sent over by Hovorka which Cunningham was relieved to slice away for a corner.

Peter McParland remembers that Northern Ireland's World Cup dream could have ended very early in this match:

> Actually, it could have been a disaster. For ten minutes the Czechs bombed us and they really tore us to pieces. Balls are flying across the goalmouth and I know Harry [Gregg] was getting a bit het up [stressed] because he

was thinking some person was not doing their job ... Had the Czechs stuck one in, in those first ten minutes it might have been a different World Cup ... But we survived that ten minutes ... and after that we held our own.

Billy Bingham believes that the team suffered from the equivalent of stagefright. 'I think, in a way, we undersold ourselves,' he reflects. 'We were better than them, but we didn't believe that until we played them.' Once Northern Ireland nerves began to settle, the pattern of play changed discernibly. Picking up the tempo, Peter Doherty's team began to break up the Czech play and switch rapidly to attack, making effective use of the long ball through the middle. As often as not, Wilbur Cush was on the end of such moves and was clearly proving a handful for Czech captain Ladislav Novak and left-half Josef Masopust. A half-chance was spurned from one attack when 'keeper Bretislav Dolejsi fumbled the ball but then gathered it safely at the second attempt.

Pushed back for a time, the Czechs put together a few good passing moves in midfield, resulting in two openings for Milan Dvorak, both of which were spurned. The Czech inside-right also forced a corner, from which Gregg made an uncharacteristic misjudgement, the ball just brushing the far post as it went wide.

These Czech attacks, nonetheless, were the exception to the pattern of the game by this stage. The momentum was with Northern Ireland and midway through the half their efforts were rewarded. From the third of three attacking moves down the flanks, McParland forced a corner on the left and took the kick quickly, passing short to McIlroy. The Burnley man's cross was a textbook kick, beating the floundering Czech defenders and finding Cush whose bullet-like header found the back of the net. The underdogs were on the way up.

The goal did not result in a change of tactics, Northern Ireland maintaining their aggressive approach, hustling their opponents into errors and when in possession, getting the ball forward as quickly as possible. In fact, just a minute after taking the lead, Northern Ireland almost netted a second. This time Cush was the provider, from a free-kick, but Peter McParland's effort was wide of the goal.

Czechoslovakia now looked vulnerable – although both Keith and McMichael had to be alert to Czech counter-thrusts down the wings – and the opportunity existed for Northern Ireland to kill the game off. Bingham and Cush were combining well on the right and chances were being created but the best of these fell to Dougan who failed to turn them into goals. In particular, one Cush pass, arguably the best of the match, gave Dougan a clear shot on goal but the ball was driven wide. The young Portsmouth forward was giving every ounce of effort but he was clearly struggling with the unfamiliar role assigned to him as a part of a dual strike force. Harry Gregg's view, however, was that playing in the World Cup 'was beyond Derek at this time', that it was just too big a challenge. 'He didn't have a particularly good game,' agrees Bingham. 'Whether the occasion got to him or not, I don't know.' The half-time whistle sounded with the score still 1-0 but with the worry lurking in the shadows that the team might still regret failing to build on that lead.

Before the game, Doherty would have been delighted with such a scoreline at the halfway stage, but now he had to take stock of a situation where the team was failing to capitalise on its superiority. The main issue was Dougan, and Doherty's solution was to give him free rein to play his normal roving game while Bingham would continue to feed Cush as a sort of combined inside-centre-forward. This would hopefully transform Dougan into a much more potent threat while maintaining the overall team pattern that had allowed Northern Ireland to establish control.

Doherty's adjustment paid dividends in the second half, at least for the first thirty minutes. Dougan's pace, and his freedom to roam, pulled the Czech defence into all sorts of uncomfortable and potentially critical contortions, keeping the initiative with Northern Ireland, if not always bringing his team-mates into the game, as Jimmy McIlroy reflects:

> I can remember, a time or two, Derek going through and me running and calling for it [but] I never seemed to get it – he just ignored me and went his own merry way sort of thing. And yet I remember thinking, 'The young so and so, he's only just in the side and he's brimming with confidence.'

Cush remained tireless as a prompter of his fellow forwards, setting up McIlroy for one shot that Dolejsi did well to save. At the back, Keith and McMichael kept the Czech wingers subdued – although outside-left Tadeas Kraus did unleash one fine shot at goal, as did Masopust – while Willie Cunningham grew in confidence at centre-half as the game progressed. He was, however, greatly assisted by captain Danny Blanchflower who, conscious that Cunningham was still finding his feet in the position normally filled by Danny's younger brother, gave the fledgling centre-half as much covering support as he could.

Of course, Peter Doherty's strategy in this match required Blanchflower to set in motion the team's attacking mechanism and in carrying this burden together with keeping close to Cunningham when it was necessary or possible, it was no surprise that the captain began to noticeably tire in the last twenty minutes of the contest.

With Blanchflower reduced to a much more limited and defensive role, so Northern Ireland gradually surrendered the initiative to the Czechs. The last quarter of the game became a backs-to-the-wall struggle to hold on to what they had. In response, the Czechs regained some spirit and hope, believing that they could salvage something from a cause that had earlier looked lost. Northern Ireland now had nine men in defence – and they needed them.

In one five-minute spell, no fewer than seven free-kicks were conceded just outside the penalty area, none more than twenty yards from goal. Gregg had to be at his sharpest to protect his goal but as he made one save after another, so one could sense a resignation spread through the Czech ranks that the Manchester United 'keeper could not be beaten. Still they attacked relentlessly but Northern Ireland defended with equal heart and held on until the final whistle brought relief, and then joy. In fact the last goalworthy shot of the match came, fittingly, from the foot of Wilbur Cush. This time he was wide of the mark, but the only goal of the game was still his to cherish.

After the match, Peter Doherty explained to the press that Northern Ireland's victory had been founded on careful planning:

> This is a triumph for our tactics. Danny Blanchflower and I saw the Czechs when they played in Copenhagen last week and we organised our strategy after that. We sent Cush and Bingham forward as a spearhead and as we had planned, our most dangerous attacks came from those tactics.
>
> We also knew that Czech inside-forward Dvorak was very dangerous with his sweeping shots, so we put Peacock on him.[4]

In Doherty's opinion it was Peacock who was the key to victory, and Blanchflower agreed that this success, for all the brilliance of Cush and Bingham up front, was one founded on solidity at the back:

I had to play more defensively than I am used to but we managed to neutralise the Czech forwards. We had expected Cush to score just in the way he did. We had been practising that tactic the whole week.[5]

Northern Ireland had started Sweden '58 as 33-1 outsiders. In beating Czechoslovakia (whose odds were just 13-1) they had made the rest of the football world sit up and take notice; as Peter McParland points out, many of these same Czech players would take their nation to the World Cup final in Chile four years later. An immediate indication of Northern Ireland's new status was an approach to the IFA by US football authorities proposing a tour of America for Peter Doherty's side at some point in the future. Northern Ireland were also able to claim the only British victory in the opening World Cup games, the other home countries all playing out draws (England 2-2 with the USSR, Scotland 1-1 with Yugoslavia, and Wales 1-1 with Hungary). Furthermore they shared top spot in their group with world champions West Germany who had beaten Argentina 3-1. In the opinion of Arthur Ellis, who had run the line in the Czech game, this standing was totally merited, as he explained to the press on the eve of the next match:

Nobody believed me when I said the Irish team is Britain's best. They have a wonderful team and fighting spirit. Gregg is fantastic. Blanchflower is in the top rank of world players. And the forwards are not to be sneezed at, as was proved on Sunday, and is likely to [be] demonstrated again tomorrow.[6]

There were then plenty of reasons to celebrate this first ever World Cup finals victory for Northern Ireland and Peter Doherty let the team do just that. In the major international football tournaments of the twenty-first century the emphasis would be on playing down the euphoria and focusing on the next game. But this was 1958 and it was also Northern Ireland in the spotlight. Peter Doherty's psychology attached importance to letting his players unwind and receiving immediate reward for what was a great victory.

That reward, again by today's standards, was quite a modest one: a night out at the local nightclub, the Norre Kat. It was a party, nonetheless, that everyone enjoyed, even Belfast's Lord Mayor, Cecil McKee, strutting his stuff and singing like Frank Sinatra (or perhaps not quite). McKee was again in attendance the next morning when the local Swedish authorities hosted a civic reception for the team at Halmstad Town Hall. A large crowd had gathered to cheer the players, strengthening the sense that Northern Ireland was 'their' team. That kind of support would be invaluable as the smallest nation in the tournament now prepared to meet the might of Argentina.

1. *Belfast Telegraph*, 3 June 1958.
2. Ibid.
3. Ibid., 9 June 1958.
4. *Irish News*, 9 June 1958.
5. Ibid.
6. Ibid., 11 June 1958.

SEVEN

DON'T CRY FOR ME

Argentina, who had qualified from a group comprising themselves, Bolivia and Chile, were the reigning champions of South America, a side of swift movement combined with unfaltering control. They could also boast of the world's most expensive player, the twenty-two-year-old Omar Sivori, who had been sold by River Plate to Juventus in Italy for £96,000; such was the talent at Argentina's disposal that he did not even make the World Cup twenty-two.

Ironically, and coincidentally considering that they were in the same group as Northern Ireland, Argentina had also come close to withdrawing from the tournament in Sweden. The issue in question was not religion but money – Mammon rather than God. The football authorities in Buenos Aires balked at the estimated cost of competing in the World Cup finals – some £30,000 – and agonised over the choice of losing face or losing finance. A climactic two-hour meeting of the Argentinian football association and senior clubs at the beginning of April finally decided to throw monetary caution to the winds and send their international team to Scandinavia. The IFA would undoubtedly have empathised with the initial financial caution if not with the ultimate risk-taking.

The opening result for Argentina – a 3-1 defeat by West Germany – could have brought succour only to the sceptics back home who had counselled against going to Sweden. Adding, as it were, injury to insult, three of the team had received bad knocks in that game – right-half Francisco Lombardo, outside-right Eliseo Prado and outside-left Osvaldo

Cruz – and were now doubtful for the critical match against Northern Ireland. Of the three, only Lombardo would line up against Peter Doherty's side.

The 3-1 scoreline and the injuries, however, did not tell the whole story of Argentina's opening game. In fact the South Americans had scored first – after just two minutes of play – and had then dominated the game, especially their wing-halfs, until about ten minutes from half-time when right-winger Helmut Rahn struck a wonder goal from twenty-three yards. Stunned by the German equaliser against the run of play – sounds familiar doesn't it? – Argentina conceded a second goal four minutes before half-time when Uwe Seeler found the net. Now in control, West Germany never looked like losing it, and a second Rahn goal, this one from thirty yards, sealed the victory at 3-1. But for more than a third of the match, Argentina had shown themselves to be a force to be reckoned with.

In terms of injuries, Northern Ireland had emerged unscathed from the encounter with Czechoslovakia but they too were considering a change to the team. Derek Dougan had not been an unqualified success at centre-forward but with Billy Simpson out of contention, the only alternative was Fay Coyle. The selectors found this decision something akin to the devil-or-the-deep-blue-sea choice, and there was even speculation that the Newcastle wing-half Tommy Casey might be given the central striking role. The final decision was in favour of Coyle, but had he been handed something of a poisoned chalice, for the Nottingham Forest player was now faced with the formidable challenge of Argentina's towering centre-half Nestor Rossi?

The Argentine central defender was one of the players who had impressed the Northern Ireland spies in the game against West Germany, the observers on this occasion being selector Sammy Walker and Linfield player-manager Jackie Milburn. 'Wor' Jackie, as the legendary centre-forward of the 1950s cup kings Newcastle United was known, knew a thing or two about centre-halfs so when he identified Rossi as a problem, Peter Doherty took notice. In Milburn's opinion, Rossi's 6ft 6in-frame offered little prospect of reward for Northern Ireland attacks down the middle of the field, advocating instead an enhanced role for the wingers to get behind the Argentinian rearguard. Doherty could see the sense in what Milburn was saying and decided to let his players get the word direct from the Linfield boss himself by inviting him to participate in the pre-match team talks.

However, another concern had been raised by the Argentinian performance against the Germans, and perhaps a more fundamental one. It manifested itself, on the surface, in a most prosaic manner: the numbers worn by certain of the Argentine team did not seem to correspond to the positions they played in. For example, the Argentinian right-half seemed to be playing at right-back. What to Milburn and Walker appeared to be a South American idiosyncrasy in fact heralded the modern age in team organisation: the 4-2-4 formation. I do not believe that Argentina can claim to be the sole originators of the new system – Brazil would employ a similar arrangement in this tournament – but this was nonetheless a bold challenge to football orthodoxy and, in this instance, a gauntlet tossed at the feet of Peter Doherty's team. In their ability to answer the challenge would lie their fate.

Danny Blanchflower sounded a note of caution on the eve of the game, particularly in relation to imposing too rigid a strategy: 'It is very difficult to plan this match because the Argentinians are so unpredictable. Anything can happen with them and we don't want to plan ourselves out of it. We are going to take an open mind ... We are best as the underdogs.'[1]

Team-mate Jimmy McIlroy, however, felt that the men in green might have a 'psychological advantage' over their opponents, 'coming in as a winning team against a side which lost'.[2] McIlroy might have done well to note the words of Argentine manager Guillermo Stabile the day before the encounter, reflecting on that opening defeat: 'We have no grumbles ... We were at full strength, so we must resign ourselves to the result. Tomorrow, we shall come again with fresh power against Ireland. We haven't lost the world with this one match. This is a series ... and we have at least two more chances.[3]

~ So it was back to the Orjans Voll stadium in Halmstad on Wednesday, 11 June for the second act in the drama of Sweden '58. Again, the local support was sure to be on Northern Ireland's side, the *Belfast News-Letter* quoting one Swedish fan remarking that, 'These are the best footballing lads we have ever had here. I wish to blazes they played in the Swedish First Division.'[4] (Did Swedish football followers really talk like that – or did the *News-Letter* need a new translator? It sounds a lot more Hillhall Road, Lisburn, than Halmstad, Sweden.)

The teams took the field before a crowd of 14,174, Northern Ireland as usual captained by Danny Blanchflower but this was a very special occasion for the Spurs right-half. Winning his thirty-second cap for his country, Blanchflower had now set a new record for international appearances for Northern Ireland, overtaking the total of goalkeeper Elisha Scott who had played for Belfast Celtic and Liverpool. Blanchflower led a side buoyed by victory over Czechoslovakia and facing a team who needed to win to keep alive their hopes of staying in the World Cup:

Northern Ireland: Gregg (Manchester Utd); Keith (Newcastle Utd), McMichael (Newcastle Utd); Blanchflower (Tottenham Hotspur), Cunningham (Leicester City), Peacock (Celtic); Bingham (Sunderland), Cush (Leeds Utd), Coyle (Nottingham Forest), McIlroy (Burnley), McParland (Aston Villa).

Argentina: Carizzo; Dellacha, Vairo; Lombardo, Rossi, Varacka; Corbatta, Avio, Menendez, Labruna, Boggi.

Before the teams took to the field, there had already been some contact, as Jimmy McIlroy remembers:

> When we lined up in the passageway to go out with the Argentinians ... and their captain looked across ... and our shorts [had a] lovely shiny, glossy [look] ... and he touched Danny's shorts and he says, 'Silk?' and then [looked] at his own shorts and said 'Cotton'.

So it was advantage Northern Ireland in the fashion department, and in fact once the game was underway, the men in the 'glossy' shorts got off to the perfect start, winning a corner on the right, which Bingham played short to Blanchflower, quite a revolutionary tactic in 1958. Blanchflower then brought Cush into the action and after an interchange of passes the Lurgan man sent over a cross which McParland headed past Amadeo Carizzo in the Argentine goal. Only four minutes of the game had elapsed and the South Americans had been caught cold.

The pattern of play for the next thirty minutes had been established, Northern Ireland attacking down the flanks to great effect, as had been planned. First Bingham and then McParland threatened to tear the Argentine defence to ribbons: the South Americans had the appearance of a punch-drunk boxer stranded on the ropes. Furthermore, Bingham and McParland also carried a goal threat when they moved inside. 'We were scoring wingers who weren't always on the wing,' states Bingham. He develops the point:

> Peter [Doherty] knew all our strengths and [how] to use them the right way. And I'd say to Peter [that] sometimes I'll finish up [a move] at centre-forward and he'd say,

'Well, stay there Bill, stay there for a little while. In the movement of the game you'll be in the centre-forward position sometimes because you're running [and] sometimes the play's on the left side and you're running in for a ball that's going to be crossed.'

A second goal for the Ulstermen looked to be on the way when Peter McParland found the goal at his mercy in the tenth minute but the man who was a hero in the fourth minute now became the villain, sending his shot wide. Nonetheless, the side was buzzing, as McParland remembers: 'We had the Argentinians on the run – we had them going.'

At the other end, Harry Gregg was continuing where he had left off against Czechoslovakia, looking agile and assured, as when he dived at the feet of the inrushing Norberto Menendez to keep his goal intact. On this solid foundation, Northern Ireland kept the flow of play heading in the opposite direction urged on by Danny Blanchflower's 'crisp through passes'.[5] A foul on McIlroy gave Bingham an opportunity for a shot on goal but he drove the ball over the bar, and another free-kick move a few minutes later was also off-target, this time from Cush. In the view of Jim Platt of the *Irish News*, 'Northern Ireland had 90 per cent of the first half-hour's play, and had been unlucky with a dozen attempts.'[6]

A second goal, indeed, might have been decisive but whether the team had burned up all its adrenalin in a frantic first half-hour of attacking, the momentum was not sustained and the balance of play began to shift. Northern Ireland started to lose their discipline, now more often resorting to attacking down the centre, instead of the wings, where their sorties usually foundered on the rock that was Nestor Rossi. Passes began to go astray, even from Danny Blanchflower who on one occasion almost cost his side a goal but for the quick reactions of Harry Gregg sprinting out to dive and gather the ball at the feet of the goal-bound Argentine forward. Captain or not, Gregg let Blanchflower know in no uncertain terms that this was not the type of play he appreciated in the last third of the pitch.

With Coyle and Cush (who had celebrated his birthday the previous day) struggling to make any impression on a solid Argentine central defence, and Bingham and McParland no longer getting the service they had earlier, the South Americans began to assert themselves, cheered on passionately by their supporters. Inside-left Angel Labruna and right-winger Omar Corbatta became imposing figures in a game which had undergone a remarkable transformation and twice Gregg had to make fine saves to keep Northern Ireland's lead intact. It was now a question of whether Peter Doherty's side could hold out to half-time and a chance to regroup.

The answer was no. With about eight minutes of the half left, Argentina attacked down the right from where Ludovico Avio sent in a swift cross seeking out Antonio Boggi. The ball skidded treacherously off the damp surface, a perilous situation for the defence, and Willie Cunningham's despairing lunge to intercept duly brought disaster. Glancing off the Northern Ireland centre-half's thigh, the ball struck his hand and all hearts stopped. The ball had clearly been handled but surely not deliberately. The Swedish referee, Sten Ahiner, did not hesitate in making his decision – a penalty-kick to Argentina.

Northern Ireland might have taken heart that the man tasked with putting Argentina level – outside-right Corbatta – was nicknamed 'El Loco' [The Madman] – but on this occasion he belied his reputation. A rock of calm in a sea of fury, El Loco struck the ball cleanly past Gregg and then let his emotions run riot. The extravagant celebrations of the South Americans was something of a culture shock to the Northern Ireland players, accustomed as they were to the muted reaction of British teams to a penalty goal when the most demonstrative gesture was usually a handshake.

Argentina were back in the game but teams are frequently at their most vulnerable when they have just scored and so it was on this occasion.

Although there were just over five minutes to half-time, Northern Ireland almost regained the lead as the South Americans momentarily dropped their guard. A slick move, starting with McMichael and involving Blanchflower, McIlroy and McParland, left Fay Coyle in on goal with time and space but he elected to hit the ball first time, sending it wide of the upright.

Amazingly with only two minutes of the half remaining, the same player missed another glorious opportunity. This time a McIlroy centre was dummied by Cush who ran over the ball, wrong-footing the Argentinian defence, leaving Coyle free to shoot on goal from about six yards. To the exasperation of team-mates and fans alike, the Nottingham Forest striker drove the ball wide. Malcolm Brodie was hardly exaggerating when he wrote: 'It was the chance of a lifetime, and one which doesn't come often in this class of football. That was, to my mind, the turning point of the game.'[7] Peter McParland's verdict on the Nottingam Forest striker – 'a near disaster' – does not appear unduly harsh.

In truth, a Coyle goal would have been against the run of play in the last fifteen minutes of the first half, only two flying saves from Gregg keeping his team on level terms at this point. Northern Ireland had lost their rhythm after the first half-hour and that pattern continued in the second half. Apart from a momentary threat when Coyle's cross almost found Cush, Argentina were now the masters. On the wings, Bingham and McParland were reduced almost to the status of spectators as Northern Ireland perversely played to the strength of their opponents, attacking down the centre where invariably the threat was quickly checked by the unyielding Argentinian central defence. The latter, in turn, became a springboard for the South Americans to launch their own offensives. As Peter McParland reflects, 'They got the penalty-kick out of nothing and they were inspired by that … they turned it on – and they were good. They give us a bit of a run-over.'

Bertie Peacock, as he had against the Czechs, worked tirelessly to keep Argentina at bay but his wing-half partner, Blanchflower, was below par, sending passes astray and failing to provide the creative impulse his team so badly needed. Playing alongside the inexperienced centre-half Cunningham was again an inhibiting factor, Blanchflower reluctant to leave the central defender exposed to the talents of the Argentine forwards; he sacrificed his normal attacking game to support his defence but this was at a considerable cost to Northern Ireland's ability to put Argentina under pressure. Arguably a free-flowing Blanchflower performance might have tipped the scales in Northern Ireland's favour, making McIlroy more assertive (though he did not play badly) and consolidating McParland's goal.

As it was, Argentina looked the more likely winners as Northern Ireland's game degenerated. Even the famous team spirit began to desert the players as they began to criticise one another, often in uncompromising language. At one point Blanchflower even felt compelled to call the team together to tell them to stop bickering as it was affecting their performance. It was symptomatic of the disharmony in the ranks in this game that they even had to be told.

Ten minutes into the second half, Argentina turned their superiority into a 2-1 lead when centre-forward Menendez finished off an incisive attacking move, assisted to some extent by poor positioning by Gregg. Football is a merciless game to 'keepers who make errors and all Gregg's impressive work up to this point was set at nought when he got caught too far out of goal, leaving Menendez with the relatively easy task of placing the ball past him from a pass by Labruna.

Northern Ireland had scarcely time to draw breath before Argentina delivered the knockout punch in the sixty-first minute. A driven cross from Corbatta evaded Gregg and was headed home from just under the bar by Avio. There was now no way back for a dispirited Northern Ireland side. Argentina continued to play with blinding speed and breathtaking control – a hallmark of their World Cup winning side of twenty years later. Even when the Ulstermen forced a couple of corners, they seemed to lack the physical strength and self-belief to put Argentina's lead under threat. In the opinion of one FIFA observer, Gustav Sebes of Hungary, 'Northern Ireland never had a chance once Argentina got into their stride.'[8]

Coyle remained ineffectual in attack, and Peter McParland, admittedly with the advantage of hindsight, regrets Doherty's selection of the Forest player: 'Thinking back ... it might have been his best bet to stick with Dougan because he might have produced,' remembering an impressive performance by the young Doog against Aston Villa at Villa Park. Contrary to Harry Gregg's opinion, McParland feels that Dougan was 'up for the World Cup' but was not given a good enough opportunity to demonstrate this. Billy Bingham does not agree, even suggesting that Dougan 'wasn't really a centre-forward' and didn't have 'a great goalscoring record'. So with one centre-forward crocked and another, who was in the opinion of one of the established members of the team, not really a centre-forward, it looked as if Northern Ireland were going to struggle to score goals, and not just in this game against Argentina.

As the match entered its closing phase, even a consolation second goal was denied Northern Ireland when Peter McParland headed over and then Cush sliced a left-foot shot inches wide of the post in the game's dying minutes. It all added up to a comprehensive defeat for Peter Doherty's men.

Yet it could all have been so different. Northern Ireland had dominated the first third of the contest and had they not lost their discipline, both collectively and individually, and not missed vital chances either side of half-time, then they might still have been top of the group. That honour now belonged to West Germany who had drawn 2-2 with Czechoslovakia. In Norman Uprichard's opinion it was more a case of Northern Ireland losing their way than having been outclassed by an Argentinian team that 'didn't impress'.

Although Peter Doherty assured the waiting journalists that: 'We can still make it,'[9] he knew that with Argentina firm favourites to beat Czechoslovakia, Northern Ireland could only reach the quarter-finals by defeating the world champions. Well, they had beaten Italy hadn't they? The Northern Ireland manager was certainly not ready to throw the towel in just yet: 'It was a little disappointing. We never think of defeat, but when it comes we can take it … [West Germany] will be a hard game … but we are in with a chance. I have great faith in the boys.'[10] A 'hear, hear' was provided by Belfast's Lord Mayor Cecil McKee, who had watched from the stands: 'We shall see more of this team. They have a good chance of getting into the next round. They were a credit to Northern Ireland.'[11]

The group table with one game left, and with only the top two teams progressing to the last eight, was as follows:

	P	W	D	L	F	A	Pts
W. Germany	2	1	1	0	5	3	3
Argentina	2	1	0	1	4	4	2
N Ireland	2	1	0	1	2	3	2
Czechoslovakia	2	0	0	1	2	3	1

Doherty might also have taken some encouragement from the fact that Northern Ireland were still the only one of the home countries with a win to their credit. In Group Four

England had played out their second draw of the tournament, 0-0 against Brazil, as did Wales in Group Three after a 1-1 result against Mexico. Scotland, however, faced an uphill task in Group Two where they were bottom of the table after losing 3-2 to Paraguay.

Northern Ireland certainly didn't give the appearance of losers when they got back to Tylösand, as Jimmy McIlroy remembers:

> When we arrived back ... we all went into the hotel and through it in a conga line, each one holding the shoulder of the one in front, singing, and the Swedes must have looked at us and thought, 'They're lunatics these paddies. They've just lost and you'd think they'd won the World Cup.' It shows you the spirit there was.

That spirit was further in evidence when the team followed the same post-match routine as after the opening game – off to the local nightclub to boogie the night away, or at least part of it. If they had lost their rhythm on the pitch, they regained it on the dance-floor, and with it a sense of being a team: a team that had climbed mountains before and was ready to do so again.

On other nights, a 10 pm curfew was in force, though it tended to be honoured more in the breach than the observation. Harry Gregg recalls one night when Peter Doherty checked with Gerry Morgan that all the players were accounted for, receiving the assurance, 'Aye, they're all in.' No sooner had Morgan spoken than the strains of 'The Sash' could be heard being whistled outside. It was Norman Uprichard. Doherty looked first at his trainer – 'Gerry, I thought they were all in?' – and then at Uprichard – 'Where have you been?' Morgan fumbled for an answer – 'Aw ... I missed that one' – but Uprichard had no hesitation in responding: 'What are you looking at me for? McIlroy's down there with a bird.' Gerry spent the rest of the evening moaning that 'that stool pigeon' (Uprichard) had let down him and his 'mate' (McIlroy).

Such incidents did not overly concern Peter Doherty for he believed in his players and in his team and this belief quickly restored team morale after the Argentina defeat. Equally, the players thought too highly of their manager ever to have thought of taking liberties. 'We would never let him down,' asserts Billy Bingham, 'he was so respected.'

Doherty was also assisted, in getting the side back on its feet, by the fans who had travelled such a long way to support their team – some larger-than-life Ulster characters. Mickey McColgan and Newry man Leslie Nicholl, for example, had shared a moped to Sweden, carrying a tent that was strapped to Mickey's back. Their tent was erected on the lawn of the team hotel where many of the players became frequent visitors, treated to tea boiled up on a primus stove. Some of the team eventually arranged for Leslie and Mickey to move into the hotel itself, displaying a bond and sense of camaraderie between players and supporters that is a million miles away from the cloistered superstardom of international football in the twenty-first century.

Mickey McColgan and Leslie Nicholl were not going to let a defeat by Argentina get them or the Northern Ireland team down. Everyone had come too far – both geographically and in terms of footballing prowess – to throw in the towel. If the World Cup holders had to be toppled, then so be it. Bring on the champions!

1. *Belfast News-Letter*, 11 June 1958.
2. Ibid.
3. Ibid.
4. Ibid.
5. *Irish News*, 12 June 1958.
6. Ibid.
7. *Belfast Telegraph*, 12 June 1958.

8. *Irish News*, 13 June 1958.
9. *Belfast Telegraph,* 12 June 1958.
10. *Irish News*, 13 June 1958.
11. *Belfast News-Letter*, 12 June 1958.

EIGHT

BRING ON THE CHAMPIONS

West Germany had produced one of the biggest upsets in World Cup history when they defeated Hungary 3-2 in the 1954 final in Berne. The 'Mighty Magyars' were the uncrowned kings of world football in the early 1950s – the side of Puskas, Hidegkuti and Kocsis; the side that had humbled England – and everyone expected the coronation to take place in the final competition in Switzerland. West Germany certainly did not seem to present a serious obstacle, swept aside by the Hungarians in the group match, the final score 8-3. In fact, West Germany only progressed beyond the group stages by defeating Turkey in a play-off game.

German teams, however, are nothing if not resilient. Despite the scale of that defeat, they recovered and applied their physical strength to good effect, overcoming one opponent after another to make it to the final. That was surely to be the limit of their success, for their opponents, Hungary, had already proved their superiority. But in a grinding encounter, in which German fitness outmatched Hungarian finesse, the World Cup was won by the country that had emerged from the ashes of World War Two.

Three of that winning side now remained to face Northern Ireland: the thirty-eight-year-old captain Fritz Walter (who had actually received the trophy from the man who had conceived the idea for such a competition, Jules Rimet); the powerful right-winger Helmut Rahn, scorer of two of the three goals against Hungary; and inside-left Hans Schaefer.

This was a solid core of experience to which was added some exciting new talent, most notably the young centre-forward Uwe Seeler. West Germany were also unbeaten in the current competition and needed only a draw to qualify for the quarter-finals, whereas Northern Ireland needed to win to be sure of staying in the World Cup. Piece of cake, then.

Unfortunately Northern Ireland did not have a Uwe Seeler at their disposal and the centre-forward spot remained a problem. The Fay Coyle experiment had not worked and now he, like Dougan after the first match, found himself discarded. The man chosen to replace Coyle was not a centre-forward – with Billy Simpson injured, Northern Ireland did not have any more – but a wing-half: Newcastle United's Tommy Casey. Casey had, in fact, been Peter Doherty's preferred choice for the centre of the attack against Argentina but he had been overruled by the selectors. Now the Northern Ireland manager was given the green light to play Casey as a deep-lying striker, à la Don Revie at Manchester City. Necessity in this case may have been the mother of innovation, but the role assigned to Casey was nonetheless an indication of both the team's and the manager's flexibility. It remained to be seen, of course, whether innovation would in turn give birth to victory.

Another handicap for Doherty's team was the venue for this last group match. The first two games had been just six miles from the team base, where they enjoyed the backing of the vast majority of the crowd: the game against West Germany was to be played in Malmö, Sweden's third city, seventy miles away and where a German support of some 10,000 fans was expected. If Halmstad had become home, the Malmö game represented an away fixture. The Swedes of Halmstad and Tylösand, however, were not about to desert 'their' team and an estimated 8,000 prepared to make the trip to cheer on Peter Doherty's side. This was no mean undertaking, for such a journey meant travelling on some of

Sweden's poorest roads and was testimony to just how much the locals had taken Northern Ireland to their hearts.

For the team itself, match day, Sunday, 15 June, began with attending a service in the church in Tylösand and then embarking on the bus. Included in the coach party were four supporters – Mick McColgan, Bill Malcolmson, Tommy Nicholl and Jack Mahood – who contributed to the high-spirited atmosphere that made the journey pass quickly. Soon the almost brand new Malmö stadium came into view.

This ground had been purpose-built for the World Cup and was hosting only its third match. The architect had come up with something of a novel design which left nearly all the crowd facing touchlines with very few places for spectators behind either goal – Billy Bingham described it as 'a diamond from which two corners had been cut off'.[1] This may have somewhat reduced the atmosphere though the Germans with their klaxon horns and the Swedes with their vocal chords still managed plenty of noise. Included too in the official attendance figure of 21,990 were a number of VIPs amongst whom were King Gustav of Sweden and the Governor of Northern Ireland Lord Wakehurst, both undoubtedly rooting for the Ulstermen if not exactly throwing toilet rolls at the German 'keeper. With the stadium bathed in sunshine and long shadows, this then was the scene that greeted the two teams:

Northern Ireland: Gregg (Manchester United); Keith (Newcastle United), McMichael (Newcastle United); Blanchflower (Tottenham Hotspur), Cunningham (Leicester City), Peacock (Celtic); Bingham (Sunderland), Cush (Leeds Utd), Casey (Newcastle Utd), McIlroy (Burnley), McParland (Aston Villa).
West Germany: Herkenrath; Stollenwerk, Juskowiak; Eckel, Erhardt, Szymaniak; Rahn, Walter, Seeler, Schaefer, Klodt.

In the previous game against Argentina, Northern Ireland got off to a dream start with a goal inside five minutes. On this occasion the same time span brought a nightmare opening when Harry Gregg twisted his ankle in one of the early tussles in the Northern Ireland penalty area. The ankle swelled up badly and if such an injury were sustained in the modern game there would be only one outcome: replacement by a substitute 'keeper. But this was 1958: there were no substitutes and equally there was no question of Gregg coming off. Instead he asked trainer Gerry Morgan to strap up the ankle with his boot still on (the only way the operation would work) and got to his feet to face the remaining eighty-five minutes as one of the walking (not yet running) wounded. Goal-kicks would now be left to his full-backs to execute. A makeshift centre-half, a makeshift centre-forward, and now a lopsided goalkeeper – not quite the ideal recipe for cooking up victory over the world champions.

If the Germans now thought that Gregg was their passport to the quarter-finals they could not have been more wrong. To say that the Northern Ireland 'keeper triumphed in adversity would be to do him an injustice – he totally dominated his penalty area, plucking crosses out of the air with a confidence that was inspiring and on one occasion even running (yes, running) outside the eighteen-yard box to head the ball clear (and in doing so, causing his cap to come down over his eyes, a cap he had been given by a workmate when he was an apprentice joiner in Coleraine and which he had salvaged from the wreckage of the Manchester United plane at Munich).

In particular, Uwe Seeler was denied by Gregg's heroics on countless occasions as the two fought out what seemed to develop into a personal duel. Twice early on the Northern Ireland 'keeper made vital saves from the young centre-forward, though on the second occasion needing two attempts to hold the ball safe. After the match Seeler acknowledged the 'keeper's world-class display: 'He seemed to be everywhere that the ball went.'[2] It was arguably the greatest game that Harry Gregg ever played. Remarkably it came after what Billy Bingham considers to have been 'two poor matches' for the 'keeper, adding that some 'thought he was going to be dropped'.

Leading from the back, Gregg's performance seemed to lift the whole team. Matching the tough tackling of their opponents, Northern Ireland also made good use of the wings, recovering the rhythm they had showed early on against Argentina. Bingham and McParland ran fearlessly at the West German full-backs, the Aston Villa man in particular proving difficult to contain and causing a buzz of anticipation in the non-German section of the crowd every time he received the ball. Bingham faced the left-back, Erich Juskowiak, who had a fearsome reputation as someone who had the strength to kick an opponent out of the ground. 'He didn't kick me over the stand,' says Bingham with a smile. 'He didn't catch me.' In midfield Jimmy McIlroy began to exhibit the class that made him one of the deadliest inside-forwards in the English First Division and looked completely at ease in competing against the champions of the world.

Peter Doherty must have been pleased too with the withdrawn centre-forward ploy which Tommy Casey was handling well – 'a destroyer in the middle of the field' is how Peter McParland describes him. The Newcastle United wing-half was more than justifying his manager's faith in him and proving to be the most effective of the three centre-forwards the team had fielded in this tournament. It was entirely fitting that he was one of the instigators of the move that saw Northern Ireland break the deadlock, though at some cost to himself and ultimately the team.

With eighteen minutes of the game gone, Casey challenged Juskowiak for the loose ball which then broke to Bingham. The winger's cross lured the German 'keeper Fritz Herkenrath to challenge Cush, the ball breaking to McIlroy who in turn pushed it into the path of McParland. The outside-left had always looked the most likely man to score for Northern Ireland and now he hammered the ball into the net. It was a remarkable goal, for all five members of the forward line had played a part.

Unfortunately Tommy Casey was in no fit state to join in the celebrations. In the challenge on Juskowiak which started off the move that led to the goal, the Northern Ireland forward had suffered a gash to the front of his right leg and had also twisted his ankle in the same incident. Casey had no choice but to come off for treatment, including strapping to the ankle and four stitches to the cut in his leg (a good advert for the wearing of shin pads which Casey wasn't). While Northern Ireland were down to ten men and within only two minutes of going behind, West Germany equalised. The scorer was the two-goal hero of the 1954 World Cup final, and the most threatening German forward on the field that day, Helmut Rahn, who produced a well-executed chip-shot to make it 1-1. Rahn had earlier powered past four opponents only to send his shot over the bar, but on this occasion the finish was pure quality.

Surely now the scales were tipped in favour of West Germany: a quick equaliser, two of the Northern Ireland team carrying injuries, and Rahn looking a menace on the right wing all added up to the Germans taking control. That was the script but Northern Ireland refused to play their part. Gregg remained a towering figure in the Northern Ireland goal while gradually Alfie McMichael got the measure of Rahn, shutting down the Germans' most threatening channel of attack, though one effort from the right-winger looked to have goal written all over it until Harry Gregg rose to palm the ball away. After the initial shock of the German goal, the Northern Ireland defence settled into a formation that looked secure and presented a formidable barrier to their opponents.

There was still the occasional close shave – as when Keith had to clear off the goal-line and Seeler miskicked in front of goal – but equally the German back line was tested by shots from McIlroy and McParland that went narrowly wide and a Peacock drive that cleared the bar. The game therefore reached half-time with the score unchanged.

During the interval, Doherty ordered a change of boots for the team (with the exception, of course, of Gregg and Casey whose boots had to stay in place) because he did not feel the rubber studs had provided enough grip. There was no change, however, to strategy – more of the same was the order of the day.

Northern Ireland maintained their momentum in the second half, especially effective down the right where Blanchflower, Bingham and McIlroy combined well to put the Germans under pressure. It is significant that this combination generated so many of the team's attacking moves – and remember, this was against the world champions – for in the opinion of one of the trio – Billy Bingham – this was the fulcrum of the Northern Ireland side. Bingham is happy to elaborate:

> I had this nice combination with McIlroy, myself and Blanchflower ... in a triangle – we were always in a triangle together [which] worked in a rotational basis in as much as Danny was a wonderful passer of the ball, and Jimmy could run with it and dribble, I could run and dribble with it and I could also go into the centre-forward position and score goals because I'd been there [as a youth player] and I knew when the centre-forward left [his position] when to run in there.
>
> [For example] I get the ball from midfield, it's hit to me by the full-back [Dick Keith] ... the opposing back's five or ten yards away from me, [so] I have a choice: I can go and try and beat him or I can go inside. Sometimes I go

inside. Now, if I go inside what's the reaction? Well, the reaction is that the inside-right [McIlroy in this case] then goes outside – you just can't run in the same channels … We were moving all the time in a solid unit. It looked as if people were losing their positions but really they were a solid unit.

Then I would go back to the right wing and again I'd start playing as a right-winger. The ball would be hit to me, I might take it to the full-back and try and get him outside or inside – try and get outside of him in particular, but if I didn't, inside I'd go, play a short ball to the centre-forward, get a return, play it to the left-winger [McParland], [then] the centre-forward moves into my position. You have to be thinking all the time [about] where you are going … Peter wanted us all working for each other, covering for each other, and just doing our defensive work and our offensive work together.

The reference to the involvement of the right-back – Dick Keith, who Bingham remembers as 'a good passer of the ball' – in this pattern of play also highlights the fact that sometimes Bingham's 'triangle' became a diamond. Keith's inclusion would often lead to the player, in Bingham's terminology, being employed on an 'interlap', that is moving forward through the right midfield channel rather than down the wing. 'We did overlaps and interlaps,' continues Bingham, adding 'I think I invented the [term] "interlap".' It was all about outwitting the opposition, something that we know had a particular appeal to Danny Blanchflower. 'McIlroy would be going round me or me going round McIlroy,' resumes Bingham, 'and interchanging, or the right-back Keith coming up, and interchanging again.'

'We played it well together and we knew each other and nobody was jealous of anybody else – there was no jealousy – so we just got on with the game.'

Apart from the reference to jealousy, which is a bit obscure, Bingham's 'insider view' illustrates vividly how fluid the team's play was under Peter Doherty, and how in this game the Germans were being tested to the limit by it. The point about the players knowing each other is also significant, and something which Bingham places much emphasis on, for Blanchflower, McIlroy, Peacock and himself had not only played together in international football for some years, but before that in club football at Glentoran.

It should also be noted that the idea of a triangle operating on the right-hand side of the field as the hub of the team will resonate with Northern Ireland fans in the current era, for they have witnessed a not dissimilar phenomenon. When the team was at its recent peak under the management of Lawrie Sanchez, beating the likes of England, Spain and Sweden, the creative heart of the side was also to be found on the right. It involved right-back Chris Baird, midfielder Sammy Clingan and winger Keith Gillespie. Their interplay was at times a joy to behold, and it now makes Billy Bingham's reminisinces come to life.

In Peter McParland's opinion, however, the real dangerman was the team's inside-right: 'Wilbur Cush came into his own in that game ... getting stuck into people. I was coming in supporting him and looking for anything that was going to drop.'

'Wilbur was like 5ft 5in,' adds Bingham, 'I think that was his height, but he was 5ft 5in broad as well. He had huge shoulders on him and the upper body of a bigger guy. He was a tremendous tackler.'

Fifteen minutes into the half this positive approach bore fruit in a second goal for Peter McParland and a quarter-final place just half an hour away. A low-swung corner from Cush was headed on by McIlroy into the path of the 'iron man' from Newry and another crashing shot bulged the German net.

West Germany now mounted an all-out assault on the Northern Ireland goal – defeat here could possibly eliminate them from the World Cup, depending on the result of the Argentina–Czechoslovakia match. In desperation they sought an equaliser but the Northern Ireland defence – Gregg in particular – remained defiant. As the minutes ticked away, the unthinkable began to seem possible.

Rahn continued to threaten on the right, Gregg on one occasion having to dive at the German's feet and push the ball clear to McMichael, while on the opposite flank Dick Keith needed all his speed to keep Bernhard Klodt in check. From one corner conceded by Keith, Gregg was content to palm the ball away for another corner but from this set piece the ball ended up in the Northern Ireland net. West German joy turned quickly to anguish when the Portuguese referee Joaquim Campos disallowed the 'goal' because of an infringement he had spotted.

Northern Ireland's forwards did their best to relieve the pressure on their hard-pressed defence, Bingham in particular grinding away on the right and having to leave the pitch for treatment after one particularly bruising challenge. Meanwhile, a Cush–McIlroy move almost produced a goal chance but Cush pushed the ball just beyond his own reach, allowing Herkenrath to intercept.

Nonetheless, the confidence and skill with which Northern Ireland were playing left the Germans beginning to look jaded as the game entered the final quarter. Danny Blanchflower's observation about the Germans as opponents seemed to be prescient, as Jimmy McIlroy recalls: 'I remember Danny saying that German football was the nearest to the British type of game. It was more robust than France or Italy – it suits us better.'

Uwe Seeler, as noted earlier, found himself foiled at every turn by the Northern Ireland 'keeper. One could have forgiven him for throwing up his hands and accepting that this just wasn't going to be his day; but that is not the German way. Just twelve minutes of the match remained when, after good work by Schaefer, the ball dropped into the path of the West German centre-forward about thirty-five yards from the Northern Ireland goal.

Gregg had looked unbeatable up to this point (apart from the isolated Rahn goal): what were the odds of beating him from this distance? Seeler even appeared to be slightly off-balance when he connected with the ball but the contact was clean and the velocity of the shot was like a missile. For once Harry Gregg was helpless as the ball flew past him into the net: 2-2. As Peter McParland remarks, 'it needed something special' to beat Gregg that day, and Seeler provided it.

This must have been heartbreaking for the Northern Ireland players – a 2-1 victory and a place in the last eight of the World Cup had been within touching distance and would not have been a travesty; but the Germans, as we have seen them do so many times, had spoiled the party. It was indicative of the team spirit in Peter Doherty's side and its footballing ability that they did not surrender but in the last ten minutes of what had been a superb game – one of the best of the tournament – fought valiantly for victory and pushed the world champions into a desperate last-ditch defence.

Indeed the Germans now paid the Ulstermen the tribute of playing for a draw, taking as much time as they could get away with over free-kicks or releasing the ball from the goalkeeper, as when Herkenrath gathered a shot from McIlroy. Right-back Georg Stollenwerk even belted the ball out of the ground to kill a few precious seconds.

In the dying minutes a flighted free-kick by Cunningham was met with the head by McParland. Fritz Herkenrath in the German goal was stranded off his line and a mere spectator as the ball went over his head. It dropped towards goal but did not drop enough, grazing the top of the crossbar and going behind, to the collective relief of the West German nation and the utter frustration of everyone in Ulster. It was the last act of a thrilling encounter, a game that was voted one of the best of the tournament.

Doherty's team left the field as heroes – almost conquerors of the world champions – but deflated in the acceptance of the reality that a draw was not good enough to keep them in the World Cup: only the miracle of a Czech defeat of Argentina could do that. Northern Ireland had seen first hand what the South Americans were capable of – they could have lost by a greater margin than 3-1 – and had little hope of any favours from Czechoslovakia. Oh ye of little faith.

Argentina did have the potential to be world beaters – as long as everything went smoothly. Faced by decisions going against them or luck appearing to desert them, they were an entirely different prospect – as Czechoslovakia proved. When the result filtered through to Malmö, it was the US Cavalry riding to the rescue of the beleaguered homesteaders: Argentina had gone down 6-1 and were out of the World Cup; Northern Ireland now faced a play-off match with Czechoslovakia to determine who would accompany West Germany into the quarter-finals. The final group table – in which only points, not goal difference, counted – was as follows:

	P	W	D	L	F	A	Pts
W. Germany	3	1	2	0	7	5	4
Czechoslovakia	3	1	1	1	8	4	3
N Ireland	3	1	1	1	4	5	3
Argentina	3	1	0	2	5	10	2

Of course if goal difference had counted, then Northern Ireland would have been out of the competition but the rules stated that those teams finishing level on points with a quarter-final place at stake would have to play an extra game. So the Ulstermen got a reprieve, but it was little more than they deserved. They had shown against West Germany that they belonged in this competition, coming agonisingly close to beating the world champions. The *Frankfurter Allegmeine* acknowledged in its comments that, 'Never before have the German observers lived through such anxiety.'[3] That was quite an admission. With his team safely through to the knockout stage, West German manager Sepp Herberger could afford to be generous to his opponents, describing Northern Ireland as 'exemplary sportsmen' who had 'played excellent football'.[4]

For its part, the press in Sweden hailed Harry Gregg as the man of the match, an opinion few would have disputed. 'Big Harry had a blinder,' was the succinct verdict of Norman Uprichard, who had watched from the sidelines. Certainly back home, Harry was a hero to the local population. People from all walks of life had got caught up in World Cup fever, telegrams flooding into the team's headquarters from individuals as diverse as the convenor of shop stewards at Short and Harland's aircraft factory, Jimmy Graham, and the cartoonist Rowel Frier who was already looking ahead to the play-off match: 'Well played. Now cross those Czechs and dislodge them.'[5]

Perhaps the simple comment of Northern Ireland's Governor, Lord Wakehurst, who, of course, had experienced all the excitement first hand, best summed up the mood in Ulster that Monday morning: 'I was so proud of them.'[6] (According to Harry Gregg, the governor had joined the team in the dressing room after the match and been offered a glass of whiskey from the trainer's bag (presumably there for medicinal purposes) – or at least what he thought was whiskey. Gregg says it was actually cold tea – someone had filched the real thing. Whether Wakehurst was too polite or too overwhelmed by the team's performance to comment we can only speculate.)

People were proud, too, that Northern Ireland were still

the only British team to have won a game in this World Cup. For the third game running, England and Wales could only draw, 2-2 with Austria and 0-0 with Sweden respectively. Both countries, like Northern Ireland, now faced play-off matches for a place in the last eight, England against Russia, and Wales against Hungary.

Sadly, Scotland were already on their way home. Their final Group Two match had ended in a 2-1 defeat by France, consigning them to bottom place and an early exit.

For Northern Ireland there was just two days to get ready for the game of their lives.

1. Billy Bingham, *Soccer With the Stars*, The Soccer Book Club, 1964, p. 118.
2. *Belfast Telegraph*, 16 June 1958.
3. Ibid.
4. *Irish News*, 17 June 1958.
5. *Belfast Telegraph*, 16 June 1958.
6. Ibid.

NINE

'YOU WERE MAGNIFICENT'

Northern Ireland had just forty-eight hours to get Harry Gregg and Tommy Casey fit for the play-off game against the Czechs – a race against time, and a short race at that.

After the West Germany game finished, Gregg and Casey were both rushed to hospital but X-rays revealed that neither had broken bones. This left at least a glimmer of hope that the players might be sufficiently healed by Tuesday but it meant a lot of hard work by all concerned. While their colleagues were allowed a well earned sleep-in on the Monday morning, Gregg and Casey underwent intensive heat treatment in room 104 of the team's hotel, under the supervision of trainer Gerry Morgan. After about two hours under the lamps, the two players moved outside to bathe their damaged ankles in the cool water of the Kattegat. The treatment was then repeated in the afternoon while the rest of the squad undertook some light training.

It was clearly an uphill battle as the team's medical attendant, Dr GS Scarlett, acknowledged to the press: 'Both are extremely doubtful, but we cannot make any decision until tomorrow.'[1] Gregg in fact remembers the initial diagnosis as ruling him out for two to three months. It all added up to more headaches for Peter Doherty, as if he didn't have enough to worry him already in terms of the opposition. Czechoslovakia's 6-1 drubbing of Argentina meant that going into this play-off, they had a decided advantage over Northern Ireland in terms of goal average

– 2 as opposed to 0.8 (goal average, for the benefit of younger readers, calculated by dividing goals for by goals against – yes, I agree, pretty daft) – and the FIFA rules stated that if the play-off ended all-square after extra time, then the quarter-final place would be determined by this method. In theory then the Czechs could progress with just a draw; Northern Ireland, on the other hand, had to win.

Doherty was also conscious that Czechoslovakia would be buoyant after their tremendous showing against Argentina when few expected them to stay in the tournament. In contrast, Northern Ireland had been within reach of the quarter-finals, only to have the prize snatched from their grasp by a late German equaliser. Now they had to do it all again: to find new physical and mental resources to take on and beat what the Northern Ireland manager acknowledged to reporters were formidable opponents: 'I think this Czech side can be devastating and it will be a hard match. They are much better footballers than the Germans, though their tackling is not nearly so hard.'[2]

Of course, it was part of Doherty's job to put his team in a positive frame of mind, so there was also a note of optimism from the manager: 'We have played better than we did against the Germans, and we hope to show the Malmoe [sic] public our top form against Czechoslovakia. We beat the Czechs last week, and why shouldn't we beat them this week?'[3]

The Czechs, however, had their own selection problems. Of their squad of eighteen players, ten were now carrying injuries picked up in the first three matches and an emergency call had to be sent out to Prague for two replacements. Team official Karel Kolsky lamented their plight but at the same time expressed their resolution on the eve of the vital eliminator against Northern Ireland:

> We can't carry on any longer like this ... Perhaps one
> or two of our injured players will recover by tomorrow,

but we can't afford to take any risk. So we have sent home for a couple of men for safety's sake. We will leave absolutely nothing to chance and are determined to beat Ireland and advance to the quarter finals.[4]

Like Doherty, Kolsky sounded both cautious and resolute:

Ireland and Germany have the same playing style – a technique which doesn't suit our style of play as well as that of the Argentinians. I'm a little worried about a number of injuries but they should clear up.
We must see how it goes, but we aim to have a stronger team out now that we have Dvorak, Hovorka, and Novak fully fit again.[5]

By Tuesday morning, matchday, Gregg and Casey were definitely ruled out of the team although even on Monday it had been clear that only a miracle could have got them fit in time. Casey pleaded to be allowed to play – no doubt prepared this time to wear a shin pad over his stitched leg – but Dr Scarlett would not sanction it. The automatic replacement for Gregg was Norman Uprichard of Portsmouth, the only other 'keeper available, who had last played for Northern Ireland in the 2-1 victory over Italy at Windsor Park in January. But who was to take Casey's place at centre-forward – the poisoned chalice in the Northern Ireland team?

Doherty had been giving the problem much thought, in consultation with Danny Blanchflower, and may well have been considering a change at number 9 even before it became a necessity. Dougan and Coyle had not measured up at centre-forward in the games against Czechoslovakia and Argentina respectively, and with Casey no longer an option Doherty conceived of the plan to play the Grimsby left-winger Jackie Scott, a former Busby Babe, in the central striking role; except that he would not stay in that position. Scott would wear the number nine shirt and line up in the centre-forward position but once the game got underway would switch with Peter McParland, the Grimsby player reverting to his accustomed club role and the Villa winger replacing him in the centre of the attack. McParland had played in a central striking role before, for Aston Villa, so this was nothing new to him, and a task he was comfortable with.

The hoped-for benefits would be confusion among the Czechs (to say nothing of the IFA selectors); more opportunity for McParland to exploit the openings fashioned by the creative talents of Blanchflower, Bingham and McIlroy; and a boost to the morale of players and supporters alike that here was further proof of the team's adaptability and flexibility at the highest level of international competition. If it did not work, of course, Northern Ireland could be out of the World Cup.

The play-off match was to be held in Malmö, the venue for the game against West Germany. This had necessitated a 140-mile round trip on the Sunday and now, two days later, Northern Ireland had to do it all again. This is where team spirit and that great sense of adventure which everyone shared compensated for the hard slog of competition. The players knew what they had to do. To paraphrase Alf Ramsey's words of inspiration to his England team before extra time was played in the 1966 World Cup final, these opponents had been beaten once; now they had to be beaten again.

The teams selected for the decisive match were the following:

Northern Ireland: Uprichard (Portsmouth); Keith (Newcastle Utd), McMichael (Newcastle Utd); Blanchflower (Tottenham Hotspur), Cunningham (Leicester City), Peacock (Celtic); Bingham (Sunderland), Cush (Leeds Utd), Scott (Grimsby Town), McIlroy (Burnley), McParland (Aston Villa).

Czechoslovakia: Dolejsi; Mraz, Novak; Bubernik, Popluhar, Masopust; Dvorak, Molnar, Feureisl, Borovicka, Zikan.

Playing before a disappointing crowd of only 6,196, the Czech line-up showed five changes from the side that had faced Northern Ireland on 8 June. Out went Pluskal, Cadek, Hovorka, Hertl and Kraus to be replaced by Bubernik, Popluhar, Molnar, Feureisl and Zikan. The match referee was to be Maurice Guigue, from France, who would later officiate in the final.

Both sides started cautiously, the Czech offensive limited to a couple of long-range shots from Titus Bubernik and Jozef Masopust, while Peter McParland forced a good save from Bretislav Dolejsi. The game then began to pick up momentum, Northern Ireland forcing a corner after a fine Blanchflower–Cush–Bingham combination, but the Czechs responded with an equally thrusting move that culminated in Jiri Feureisl volleying just wide with his left foot. A Milan Dvorak free-kick threatened danger for a moment but the Northern Ireland defensive wall proved equal to the challenge.

Nonetheless, for the first eight or nine minutes everything went according to Doherty's plan – the Scott/McParland switch bewildered the Czech defence and seemed to hand Northern Ireland the attacking initiative – but then the injury hoodoo struck again. Northern Ireland had just come close to scoring from a well rehearsed free-kick just outside the Czech penalty area, McIlroy running over the ball and Bingham chipping a pass to Scott whose goal effort was just inches wide.

From the resultant clearance, the Czechs pressed down on the Northern Ireland goal and as Norman Uprichard came out to gather the ball he slipped and twisted his right ankle, a similar injury to that sustained by Harry Gregg, the man he had replaced, in the German match.

Uprichard's response was also in line with Gregg's – pick yourself up, dust yourself down and start all over again – an inspiration to his team and the people supporting from the sidelines. Northern Ireland continued to attack and put their opponents under pressure, although the flow of the match was upset by a series of free-kick awards. A goal looked likely and it came in the seventeenth minute; unfortunately for the team doing most of the attacking, it was scored by Czechoslovakia.

There did not appear to be any particular danger from the Czech centre-half Jan Popluhar's high ball into the Northern Ireland penalty area, even though it did evade Willie Cunningham. Dick Keith seemed to have matters under control – that is until he was bundled aside by Borovicka. The referee waved play on as the ball reached the head of outside-left Zdenek Zikan, who up to this point had been kept quiet by Keith's excellent tackling, and he guided it past the helpless Uprichard. Totally against the run of play, the central Europeans were in the lead and facing a team with an injured 'keeper.

The goal might have proved a turning point in favour of the Czechs but, as noted before, Peter Doherty's team believed in itself and refused to panic or surrender. Good football was the order of the day and that is what the players continued to provide, none more so than Danny Blanchflower, in this game truly playing a captain's part as he engineered attack after attack. Losing the self-imposed inhibition that had cramped his style in the earlier games, primarily because of concern about the inexperience of Willie Cunningham as a centre-half, the Northern Ireland right-half now gave rein to his natural attacking game, acknowledging too that a defensive approach would not turn around a 1-0 deficit. Billy Bingham recognises just how important an in-form Blanchflower was to his side:

> Danny was basically an attacking player and liked to change the game from right to left [or vice versa]. He liked to slot balls through the middle to the centre-forward. He was very skilful on the ball ... He was [also] a brilliant tackler, a low tackler, to take the ball. But he had no speed – he could be licked like that [Bingham snaps his fingers]. That was his biggest weakness, I would say, as a player. Now, all the other things that he had somehow shadowed that. He was so good at slow tackles ... at creative play, sliding the ball through.

Taking their lead from Blanchflower, Northern Ireland's forwards applied relentless pressure on the Czech goal but an equaliser remained elusive. It almost came just before the half-hour but an indirect free-kick in the Czech penalty area for once found McParland slow to get his shot in. Then a long ball out of defence from Dick Keith was flicked on by Cush to McParland whose lay-off to McIlroy in front of goal seemed to augur the breakthrough at last only for the Czechs to muster a last-ditch clearance.

At the other end, Uprichard, à la Gregg, and despite his ankle injury, came out of his penalty area to clear the ball with his head, and not to just anywhere but safely to his colleague Dick Keith. From there, Northern Ireland could again begin an offensive.

The referee was already looking at his watch, with just about one minute of the first half left to play, when Billy Bingham mounted yet another assault down the right wing. Sprinting wide of the Czech defence, the Sunderland winger's cross found Cush in space and with a chance to shoot on goal. His first-time effort was blocked by Dolejsi's feet, and two follow-up shots were also parried away. Cush, however, was still in there fighting, but now spotted McParland in a better position and squared the ball to the decoy centre-forward. The Villa man needed only the one chance to drive the ball home for the most timely of equalisers. Fate had smiled at last: the half-time whistle sounded before the game even got restarted.

The smile, however, was a fleeting one. When play resumed, Uprichard had to go through the pain barrier again. Diving to turn away a shot from Dvorak, the Northern Ireland 'keeper smashed a hand against the upright (according to the newspapers, but the goalkeeper is adamant that someone kicked him) but like his earlier injury, shook it off to play on. It was only after the game that it was discovered that the hand was in fact broken. (It was at least fortunate that it was not the same hand that Derek Dooley of Sheffield Wednesday has almost smashed to a pulp in Uprichard's early days at Portsmouth.) A 'keeper with only one good hand and one good foot ...

Under Peter Doherty, Northern Ireland's natural inclination was always to attack but now there was the added motive of wishing to keep the ball as far away as possible from the hobbling Uprichard. When the Czechs did threaten the Northern Ireland goal, the outfield players did everything possible to protect their injured goalkeeper but this too had its risks, as Bertie Peacock learned to his cost. The Northern Ireland left-half got caught up in one multiple collision in his own penalty area, also involving Uprichard and the Czech goalscorer Zikan, which left him nursing a badly injured leg. In fact, his knee had locked and he had torn ligaments – in trying to shield his goalkeeper, the Celtic man had ended up just as badly injured as Uprichard. For the rest of the game, Peacock was little more than a spectator, though he was never completely out of the action. This was a serious blow to Northern Ireland, for Peacock had been one of their stars in this competition, Peter McParland judging him to be 'our best player during the tournament'.

Just moments after Peacock's injury, Feureisl pulled a muscle trying to execute a scissors kick and also had to leave the field for treatment. Norman Uprichard, meanwhile, struggled on, pulling off a daring save at the feet of Pavol Molnar and palming away a Zikan shot at the end of a swift Czech counterattack after a Peter McParland thunderbolt at the other end. Well might Peter Doherty have admired his 'keeper's endurance, describing it later as 'one of the most courageous things I have seen in a football match'.[6] It was hardly an exaggeration.

Amazingly, despite being down to only nine fit players, Northern Ireland remained the dominant force in the game. Cush was outstanding in finding time and space to bring his fellow forwards into the game, McIlroy ending one such move with a disappointing shot straight at the 'keeper. Dolejsi, however, was certainly earning his match fee, with save after save, one particularly noteworthy effort being a magnificent leap to claim the ball from Blanchflower's lofted free-kick. Such was the pressure from the men in green, indeed, that the Czechs' first priority was no longer free-flowing football, as the correspondent of the *Irish News* noted: 'Bingham and Cush had the Czech defence in a tangle and were beating their men at will, being stopped only by shirt-pulling and obstruction.'[7] McParland also remained a constant threat, as he 'floated in and out' between the left wing and the centre-forward position, maximising his team's attacking options and maximising the confusion among their opponents.

With fourteen minutes left to play, McParland dummied a through ball to let it pass to Scott but the latter hesitated and the opportunity was wasted. Arguably, the best effort at goal in the second half came from a Billy Bingham header which had the Czech 'keeper well beaten but came back off the crossbar. Fittingly, the ninety minutes drew to a close with Doherty's team on the attack, left-back Alfie McMichael sending into the Czech penalty area what the *Irish News* described as a 'long, swinging drive'.[8] At full-time the game remained – like Bertie Peacock's knee – deadlocked.

In the few minutes of respite before extra time commenced, Peter Doherty had some major surgery to perform on his damaged team. One proposal that was point blank refused was to have Uprichard taken to hospital to have his hand put in plaster; a sensible idea but one to which the Northern Ireland 'keeper would not agree. He was not going to abandon the team in their hour (or half hour) of need. He even offered to play on the wing if needs be. Doherty could only acknowledge Uprichard's courage and commitment. Whether Gerry Morgan's somewhat unorthodox treatment of the goalkeeper's ankle injury – pouring whiskey over it – kept Uprichard in the game must remain open to question. Uprichard himself remains sceptical 'What a waste of good whiskey' he sighs.

Elsewhere in the team, positions were switched to accommodate Bertie Peacock's reduced mobility. The versatile Wilbur Cush was moved back to left-half and Peacock put on the left wing. Jackie Scott, who had been playing in that position now switched wings while Billy Bingham moved to the inside-right slot vacated by Cush. It was not so much plan B as plan Z.

What the Czechs would make of the rearranged opposition remained to be seen, but they could not have but been impressed, and perhaps, demoralised, as the Northern Ireland team started exercising before the game got underway again. This was a spur-of-the-moment suggestion by Billy Bingham who thought it might just give Northern Ireland a psychological advantage over their opponents. It certainly didn't do any harm. Bingham relishes the memory:

> I did this spontaneously … I was trying to think of the best way to win the game … They [the Czechs] went and lay down on the ground, all of them … I don't know whether psychologically it [had] an effect … but I would have thought so. I was really hyped up … [as if saying to

> my colleagues] 'Let's scare the shit out of them.' ... I was
> a hard trainer all my life. A lot of the guys I played with
> [again unnamed] didn't train hard ... they wanted the
> easy way out.

So, apparently, did the Czechs, as they lay and watched the mad Ulstermen use up valuable energy.

Northern Ireland were also bolstered by the support from the crowd where a Royal Navy contingent were making their presence felt in cheering on Doherty's team and where even a few Germans were shouting for the Ulstermen. The vast bulk of support, of course, was not at the stadium in Malmö but back home in the Emerald Isle. It was estimated that in Northern Ireland 250,000 people were listening to the game on the BBC Home Service (this before the days of Radios 1, 2, 3, 4, and 5 Live), most of whom must have been aghast when the commentary was interrupted for the 9 pm news. One disgruntled caller got through to the BBC's Northern Ireland sports editor, Charles Freer, who tried to offer an explanation of BBC policy on broadcasting the news. Freer was interrupted by the caller's concluding and unanswerable comment: 'News, catch yourself on man – if Northern Ireland has beaten Czechoslovakia this evening 'twill be the biggest news since the Relief of Mafeking.'[9]

If Northern Ireland's task was not quite as daunting as trying to recover a town surrounded by enemy forces in the South African War at the beginning of the century, then the Czech mission was even less intimidating. The Czechs knew that if they could hold on to what they had – a 1-1 draw – for another thirty minutes then they would qualify for the World Cup quarter-finals on goal average. For Northern Ireland, as was to be the case against host nation Spain in the 1982 World Cup, only victory would do.

So battle was rejoined in what amounted to a survival of the fittest, and as Peter McParland recalls, his colleagues did not flag but rather 'battled like hell'. Ten minutes into the first period of extra time, Northern Ireland won a free-kick on the right, halfway into the Czech half of the field. Danny Blanchflower stepped up to take the kick, though, as he later recalled, he had very little left to give:

> I was ragged and tired as I went to take it. I recall urging myself that I must concentrate all the more and try and get it to McParland which was one of our tactics at the time. With great deliberation I took the kick and it went away ever so sweetly right to the spot I had intended.[10]

It was a move the players had practised in training and its execution was perfect. Blanchflower later acknowledged this as one of the best free-kicks he had ever taken, floating the ball to McParland whose crashing right-foot volley found its mark. It was the Aston Villa winger's fifth goal in four games and it left Northern Ireland just twenty minutes from the quarter-finals of the World Cup. McParland was turning out to be Northern Ireland's secret weapon in this World Cup, dovetailing with the 'creative department' on the right-hand side, as Billy Bingham explains:

> McParland [also linked into] the build-up on the right-hand side ... McParland was doing some good things on the ball with Peacock's passing and the left-back's passing, who at that time was Alfie McMichael, but when the play was developing on the right side, through McIlroy, Blanchflower and myself and the right-back, Keith, what was happening then was, the service coming over, and if you could get that service to McParland, who was 5ft 11in, rakey, could head a ball, whack it in with his left foot or right foot at the far post, [you got results]. It was a creative thing on our right side [and McParland] was getting on the end of those [moves] ... Peter benefited

by the fact that we were punching holes [in the defence] on the right side.

Both of McParland's goals in this game had come from play on the right, and Bingham uses a modern illustration to give one a mental picture of a Peter McParland goal, referring to Michael Owen's headed goal for Newcastle against Sunderland at St James' Park on 20 April 2008, featured on BBC's *Match of the Day*. Owen had come in behind the Sunderland defence from the left to meet a cross played from the right-midfield position. That was a Peter McParland goal.

For Czechoslovakia, 6-1 victors over Argentina, that second goal from the real Peter McParland was a devastating blow from which they never recovered in this game. Just a few minutes after conceding the second goal, the Czechs found themselves down to ten men when one of their star players, right-half Titus Bubernik, was sent off for spitting in the face of the referee. Claiming variously that he was reacting to a foul by an opponent and that, as Peter McParland overheard, 'I was spitting just as the referee was passing me,'[11] (surely the most unfortunate case of being in the wrong place at the wrong time), referee Guigue had no hesitation in dismissing a player who had clearly broken under the pressure. With discipline gone, the game itself slipped beyond the reach of Czechoslovakia.

While the second period of extra time was agony for the watching fans and officials, on the field Northern Ireland did not look in any serious danger. In fact, they managed to put the ball in the Czech net for a third time but Bertie Peacock's effort – yes, the one-legged novice winger – was ruled out for offside against Jackie Scott. It was a shame that the goal did not stand, for Peacock had been a true hero while his footballing performance in this match, in the opinion of the *Irish News*, had established him as 'one of the finest half-backs in the tournament'.[12]

Still the final whistle did not sound, and Harry Cavan, one of the selectors who like all the IFA officials and local pressmen had come down to the touchline, simply could not bear to watch. Finally the whistle blew and the miracle was complete – Mafeking had been relieved.

Northern Ireland were joined in the last eight of the 1958 World Cup by only one other British team, fellow minnows Wales. While England had lost their play-off match against Russia by 1-0, the Welsh had beaten Hungary 2-1, though the crowd of just 2,823 was the lowest recorded at a World Cup finals since the first competition in Uruguay in 1930. That hardly mattered to Wales or Northern Ireland, both of whom were now just two games away from the final of the World Cup.

At the end of their game the Northern Ireland players had been mobbed by their fans, the IFA officials and the newspaper reporters from home. The pandemonium carried on into the dressing room – it was like Christmas, birthdays and winning the national lottery rolled into one. The noise of celebration was only stilled temporarily to hear a few words from the man who had guided Northern Ireland to this moment of glory. Few words were necessary on such an occasion but perhaps Peter Doherty's salute was all the more memorable for that very reason: 'Well done, boys. You were magnificent.'[13]

1. *Belfast Telegraph*, 16 June 1958.
2. Ibid., 17 June 1958.
3. *Belfast News-Letter*, 17 June 1958.
4. *Irish News*, 17 June 1958.
5. *Belfast News-Letter*, 17 June 1958.
6. *Irish News*, 18 June 1958.
7. Ibid.
8. Ibid.
9. N Ireland v. England, Windsor Park, Belfast, 4 October 1958, official match programme.

10. Danny Blanchflower, *The Double and Before ...*, Nicholas Kaye, 1961, p. 165.
11. Peter McParland, *Going for Goal*, Souvenir Press, 1960, p. 69.
12. *Irish News*, 18 June 1958.
13. *Belfast Telegraph*, 18 June 1958.

TEN

PATCHED UP, BUT FULL OF PRIDE

Again, Northern Ireland had only two days to recover before their quarter-final match – against Group Two winners France in Norrköping. This would be the Ulstermen's third game in five days, their fifth in twelve. This would have been a daunting challenge for a fully fit side but Northern Ireland were far from that at this stage of the competition.

The injury list was now approaching epic proportions, the casualties comprising Norman Uprichard with a twisted ankle and broken hand; Harry Gregg with a badly swollen ankle; Bertie Peacock with torn ligaments in the left knee; Alfie McMichael with a bruised thigh and leg; Willie Cunningham with a bruised foot; Peter McParland with a similar injury to Cunningham; Wilbur Cush with a bruised arm; and of course Billy Simpson with his pre-tournament pulled muscle. Of the squad of seventeen, only nine were not receiving treatment. Little wonder that Billy Bingham – one of the uninjured – surveying the scene at Tylösand the day after the play-off match, compared it to 'a hospital ward, with Dr Scarlett and Gerry Morgan toiling ceaselessly with intensive heat treatment, hot fermentations and dressings for cuts and abrasions'.[1]

In fact Morgan and Scarlett were glad to get help from a Swedish masseur and even one of the Northern Ireland supporters. Billy Malcolmson had initially been adopted by the team as an assistant bagman to Gerry Morgan, but now he also was employed as a masseur (though it is not clear what his qualifications in this field were, other than availability). It was another example of how Northern Ireland's challenge in the 1958 World Cup embraced everyone – players, officials, reporters and supporters – operating as one big happy family.

That family also included the team's unofficial mascot, young Bengt Jonasson. He played his part, too, coming to the rescue when Billy Bingham could not get a worn stud out of his boot with only three hours to kick-off. Bengt sallied off to a shoe repairer in the town, got the boot fixed and returned in time and in triumph.

The spirit may have been willing but unfortunately the flesh was weak, and in some cases weaker than others. Both of the goalkeepers available were injured but with a broken bone in the hand, Norman Uprichard was totally out of the running. First-choice 'keeper Harry Gregg's injury would in normal circumstances have meant an eight-week lay-off – instead he was forced to return after just four days. Discarding the walking stick he had been using, Gregg underwent intensive treatment: alternately bathing the damaged ankle in the sea for a few hours and then having it subjected to an infra-red lamp in the team hotel (he recalls spending so much time in the water that he was numb from the waist down). Peter Doherty was not being entirely facetious when he remarked that 'Gregg will play if we have to carry him on,'[2] and the 'keeper himself maintains that he 'would have played on crutches'. Norman Uprichard says simply that 'Harry had to play with one leg'.

Bertie Peacock, like Uprichard, was a non-starter for the France game (and would in fact be out of action for three months), so Wilbur Cush had to remain at left-half. This meant a vacancy had to be filled at inside-right and the man chosen was Tommy Casey who was still nursing a severe leg wound from the game against West Germany. (The wound would re-open in the quarter-final match and Casey would end the game with his sock soaked in blood.) Casey may only have had one sound leg but he obviously had plenty of balls.

Three games in five days and a crippled squad: could Northern Ireland be lumbered with any more handicaps? Well, er … yes. What about a ten-hour 200-mile coach journey to get to the stadium in Norrköping? Having won their group while Northern Ireland came second in theirs, France were entitled to stay at the same venue that had hosted all their group games, so there could not be any complaints on those grounds. However, the Norrköping trip came on the back of an intensive bout of long-distance travel to matches for Peter Doherty's side that smacked of bad planning. The game against France was to be played on Thursday, 19 June.

The previous Sunday Northern Ireland had made a 140-mile four-hour round trip for the final group match against West Germany in Malmö; two days later the journey was repeated for the play-off match against Czechoslovakia. Furthermore, the team did not leave Malmö until three in the morning after the game as they had to wait on Uprichard returning from the hospital. Getting to Norrköping for the quarter-final would mean the team had clocked up close to 600 miles (by coach, remember) in the space of five days, equating to eighteen hours on the road. This was no way to handle a team already fatigued by intensive competition on the football field.

Instead, the team could have stayed in Malmö after the West German game to face Czechoslovakia on the Tuesday and then flown from Malmö to Norrköping. Of course this would have meant additional expenditure but then what price do you put on a place in the World Cup semi-finals? Obviously not too high a one if you are with the IFA. Jimmy McIlroy, however, is philosophical about the matter, putting it down to perhaps naivety on the part of FIFA: 'The World Cup wasn't in its infancy but wasn't anything like as organised as it is today.'

Billy Bingham simply remarks that 'things could have been done better' but acknowledges that he only 'felt it afterwards'.

Certainly the issue about all the travelling was never raised at the time and there were no grumbles from any of the team. Indeed, Wilbur Cush phoned his fiancée Joyce Reid in Aghalee to say that all the players were in great heart. There was a festive atmosphere at the team hotel in Tylösand, all the staff waving and cheering as the bus pulled out for the long journey. The songs and the jokes on board would help cut the miles and the hours but it was still a trek the team could have done without.

The faithful few were, of course, among the 11,800 crowd in the Norrköping stadium to cheer the team on, but back home the interest in the game was reaching, well, fever pitch. Again, radios were expected to be tuned in all over Ulster as the BBC Home Service prepared to broadcast the match between 7.00 pm and 9.00 pm. The game happened to coincide with a by-election for Belfast Corporation (forerunner to Belfast City Council) in the Victoria ward, and politics was expected to lose to sport in terms of turnout. As a City Hall spokesman observed, 'I am sure there will be very few men anxious to leave their seats until nine o'clock and the polling stations close at 8.30.'[3] Interest was just as great across the border, Councillor McLaughlin from Buncrana in County Donegal noting that Northern Ireland's exploits were creating 'wild interest'[4] ('wild' used in the Ulster sense of 'tremendous').

Meanwhile, back in Sweden, although his side scarcely needed motivating in a World Cup quarter-final, Peter Doherty did remind the players about their likely opponents if they got to the semi-final: 'You know what's down the road after this ... the circus act.' The circus act was Doherty's euphemism for Brazil, whose bag of tricks on the field did not always impress the manager, as Peter McParland remembers.

Did Doherty fancy his team's chances against the South Americans? Norman Uprichard maintains that he certainly 'wanted a dig at them'. First things first, of course, and before any game against the South Americans, there was formidable opposition to be faced in the shape of France.

As well as having what amounted to 'home' advantage in this quarter-final tie, France had also had four days to recuperate from their final Group Two game – as Peter McParland puts it, 'They were sitting up for five days waiting for us to come' – reflected in the fact that the side was unchanged from that game, a 2-1 win over Scotland. It was the athletes against the invalids, the teams lining up as follows:

Northern Ireland: Gregg (Manchester Utd); Keith (Newcastle Utd), McMichael (Newcastle Utd); Blanchflower (Tottenham Hotspur), Cunningham (Leicester City), Cush (Leeds Utd); Bingham (Sunderland), Casey (Newcastle Utd), Scott (Grimsby Town), McIlroy (Burnley), McParland (Aston Villa).
France: Abbes; Kaelbel, Lerond; Penverne, Jonquet, Marcel; Wisniewski, Fontaine, Kopa, Piantoni, Vincent.

Northern Ireland, as was to be expected in the circumstances, adopted a defensive pose, hoping to catch their opponents on the break – they simply didn't have the resources now to play their normal attacking game. Nonetheless, Blanchflower and Cush sent penetrating passes forward from both flank half-back positions and in an early attack Bingham and McIlroy combined on the right wing but the Burnley man's cross was dealt with comfortably by Claude Abbes. Peter McParland also remembers coming close in the early stages: 'I belted a header from the six-yard line and the 'keeper knew nothing. We could have gone one up. He put his arm out.' The save was instinctive and the ball was deflected behind the goal and to safety. It was a sparkle of hope on an overcast day, but France were an attacking team and soon they were on the offensive.

Juste Fontaine, one third of the formidable central attacking force that comprised himself, Raymond Kopa and Roger Piantoni, gave the Northern Ireland defence a taste of things to come with a dribble along the touchline that left three men in his wake. The final cross was captured by Harry Gregg but the respite was only temporary. The French left-half Jean J Marcel began to make his presence felt with a couple of powerful shots, the first of which floored Wilbur Cush (no mean achievement) and the second evading Gregg's grasp, leaving the Northern Ireland 'keeper to dive at the feet of Jean Vincent to clear the ball.

Serious questions were now being asked of the Northern Ireland defence but so far they were still managing to come up with the answers. Dick Keith was certainly an inspiration to his team-mates with some effective tackling although he was little more than a spectator to Piantoni's mazy run that took the French inside-left past four defenders but again failed to produce the breakthrough. Kopa, too, was a constant threat, Gregg twice having to come off his line to claim the ball off the head of the Gallic centre-forward.

Blanchflower out of necessity was devoting more time to assisting the defence but when opportunity arose was still feeding excellent passes through to the Northern Ireland forward line, Jim Platt, of the *Irish News*, counting at least twenty such in the first fifteen minutes alone. McIlroy also drove in a fierce shot which Abbes could only parry. But the French defence was mobile and, when it needed to be, hard as rock, witness McIlroy's felling by Marcel or Jackie Scott's upending in the French penalty area in the thirteenth minute. Appeals for a penalty did not sway Spanish referee Juan Gardbazalbal who signalled for play to continue.

Approaching the mid-point of the first half, the game had settled into a clear pattern: France were the team with the best ball control and individual flair but Northern Ireland were stronger in the tackle and seemed to have more energy in attack, especially from Jimmy McIlroy. There continued to be occasional scares for Peter Doherty's men, as when Cush slipped when trying to tackle Fontaine in the seventeenth minute, a potential catastrophe only averted by Gregg's swift sortie out from his goal-line; or seven minutes later when Fontaine's header came back off the bar and Armand Penverne sliced a follow-up shot well clear of the goal from eight yards.

Four minutes later, Tommy Casey came just as close to a goal at the other end of the field, picking up a loose ball from Scott's corner-kick but sending his shot just wide of the upright. With Northern Ireland growing in confidence, Casey turned creator with a cross that eventually found its way to Bingham but again the final shot was just off-target.

By the later stages of the first half, Northern Ireland were in the ascendant, Blanchflower and Cush acting as springboards for thrusts down the wings or via McIlroy in the more central channel. As they had done in the play-off match against Czechoslovakia, McParland and Scott had switched position though the Villa man might have been employed to greater effect on the flank, running at the opposition and attacking from their blindside, the French being focused on the threat from Bingham on the right. Indeed, just ten minutes from half-time a typical four-man move gave the Northern Ireland outside-right a chance for a header on goal but he was denied by Michel Lerond who up to that point had usually come off second best against Bingham.

When Northern Ireland won a throw-in on the right, level with the French eighteen-yard line, an opportunity presented itself to apply a move the team had practised a number of times. The plan was for Blanchflower to throw the ball to Bingham's head who would then flick it on to McIlroy. The ball indeed reached the Burnley player via this route, clear for a shot at goal but he hesitated and was then forced into a square pass which the French cleared. It was an incident that in some ways encapsulated Jimmy McIlroy's World Cup, as he now reflects:

> It embarrasses me when I look at the five games [in the World Cup] and find that I didn't score ... [I often] panicked in front of goal – even in a five-a-side – and yet at the other end of the field, [on] my own eighteen-yard line or six-yard line, I could dribble the ball out full of confidence ... When I had to finish off a move I was never as cool as I should have been ... All my football career I never considered myself a goalscorer ... [but] I tried to make as many goals as I could ...

It is a very candid assessment but while he may not have got the goals himself, his presence and threat undoubtedly contributed to the team's success. While not denying the Burnley man's positive contribution throughout, Billy Bingham feels that McIlroy did not do himself justice in the competition. 'He didn't have a great World Cup,' he reflects, 'he never struck great form – steady, but he never struck [the] great form which we knew he was capable of.' McIlroy's missed chance may well have been the game's pivotal point, although it is perhaps harsh to burden him with this responsibility retrospectively.

Nevertheless, the fact was that despite the number of attacking moves Northern Ireland put together, they failed to draw first blood (unless you count Tommy Casey's leg) and instead the game turned in the opposite direction. With two minutes left of the first half, France sent what was by now a rare attack into the Northern Ireland penalty area where the defence, perhaps with their minds already in the dressing room, reacted like a pin-ball machine until the ball reached the feet of French outside-right Maryan Wisniewski who drove his shot into the far corner of the net under Gregg's despairing dive.

It was the perfect time to score; the worst moment to concede a goal. The second half now threatened to be an uphill struggle for Northern Ireland but it turned out to be even worse.

Northern Ireland started the second half with a flurry of attacks. Bingham was playing his heart out on the right wing and after dispossessing Lerond, sent in a driven cross which outpaced the French defence but unfortunately also the rest of the Northern Ireland attack – one touch could have brought the scores level. Another good chance was spurned in the fifty-second minute when a quick Cush free-kick found McIlroy slicing at thin air with the goal at his mercy from six yards out.

Cush, however, was destined to play a part in the game's second goal, though not in the manner he would have wished. Within four minutes of setting up the McIlroy chance, the Glenavon captain dispossessed Wisniewski near the Northern Ireland left corner flag but then mishit his clearance straight to Penverne, standing only five yards away. The French right-half's cross was inch-perfect, picking out the unmarked Fontaine whose header into the top left-hand corner of the goal gave Harry Gregg no chance.

Peter Doherty's men were down but not out and rallied to the challenge. However, with a two-goal advantage, France had a sharpness now which they had lacked in the first half, best personified by their centre-forward, Real Madrid's Raymond Kopa.

He it was who conducted the French orchestra to produce football of beauty and simplicity and who in the sixty-fourth minute sent through a perfectly weighted pass to Fontaine who beat two men, drew Gregg out of his goal and then unleashed a low shot to make the score 3-0. It was Fontaine's second goal of the game and his eighth of the tournament – he would eventually end up as top scorer with thirteen.

Again McIlroy might have pulled a goal back but he failed to convert Bingham's pass along the six-yard line. As if to confirm that this was not Northern Ireland's day, France swept to the other end where Piantoni caressed the ball down the right touchline, cut inside past Cunningham and then drove an unstoppable shot past Gregg high into the net and just inside the near post. There were still twenty-two minutes of the match left but there was no doubt now about who was destined for the semi-final.

Northern Ireland kept competing and only an offside decision denied McIlroy a goal, which surely his efforts throughout the competition merited, and then a Wilbur Cush shot seemed to have goal written all over it until a French defender got in the way. It was not to be. The final whistle blew at last: this time it really was all over for Peter Doherty's team.

Yet Northern Ireland were beaten as much by sheer fatigue and injury as by the footballing prowess of France. In Jimmy McIlroy's opinion, the team 'just ran out of steam, and at the end, I think, we were just glad to hear the final whistle because we actually were exhausted'. It was hardly a coincidence that all the teams that had had play-off matches lost their quarter-finals (including Wales, 1-0 to Brazil, the goalscorer Pelé) – they simply had not had time to recover.

A fully fit and rested Northern Ireland would have produced a very different game and probably a very different result. Malcolm Brodie, of the *Belfast Telegraph*, and inside-forward Jimmy McIlroy, who had missed his team's best chances, were convinced that what Brodie referred to as a 'fit and fighting'[5] Northern Ireland would have beaten France. Northern Ireland had arguably played better sides in their group and had emerged triumphant. The 4-0 scoreline was not a true reflection of either team's capabilities. IFA Secretary

Billy Drennan may not exactly have been a disinterested observer of events, but his summing up of this game and the team's overall showing in the tournament seemed well-founded:

> It was fatigue and not football that beat our boys in the end. They carried many scars of battle, but had they had another day between the play-off with Czechoslovakia and the French match I believe Northern Ireland would have been ... in the semi-finals.
>
> As it is, we are now graded among the best in the world, and as well as giving a boost to British football the team won the admiration of all Sweden. They were certainly a grand advertisement for Northern Ireland.[6]

As ever, Norman Uprichard cuts right to the heart of the topic, reflecting that 'through injuries and tiredness, Dundela would have beat us', making reference to the 'Duns' who are now members of the Irish League First Division (second tier of Irish football) but in 1958 competed in Irish intermediate football.

Billy Bingham, however, does not subscribe to what appears to be the consensus view that Northern Ireland had simply 'ran out of steam':

> They do say that when they get licked – they tend to say that ... I think it had been so close in all those matches – I mean there wasn't [sic] any easy matches at all – and then you were getting near to what I would call the apex of the tournament, and then you're meeting more quality and I think that quality was in France ... Without making excuses, France were better on the day ... We weren't the best side in the tournament; we had a nice mixture of determination, skill certainly, but not as skilful as [France or Brazil] would have been. [But] some of them mightn't

have had our determination. That determination gets you a fair distance but sometimes it isn't just enough to get you to the final. We had four or five players who could have been picked for the best team.

Bingham's reflections on defeat initially seem to argue that there was a gulf in class between the sides, but then seem to veer away from that conclusion. Nonetheless, his essential point – that Northern Ireland had been well beaten on the day – is not open to contention.

Equally, that defeat has to be put in the context of a wonderful performance overall in the competition, which was the note struck by the Northern Ireland Prime Minister Lord Brookeborough in his telegram to team captain Danny Blanchflower: 'Northern Ireland is proud of your magnificent performances in the World Cup. My heartiest congratulations on your fine sportsmanship in defeat as in victory. It was a splendid effort by players and officials alike.'[7] Belfast Corporation was already planning a civic reception for the team on their return.

Tributes were showered on Peter Doherty's side, including one from Lady Wakehurst, wife of the Governor of Northern Ireland. She had been on holiday in Scandinavia and on her return to Ulster had remarked on how the team's World Cup adventure had done more to promote Northern Ireland 'than anything else we could possibly have done'.[8] She went on to comment:

> There was something very attractive about the team. They had a universal appeal throughout Scandinavia ... Everywhere we went people asked us questions about Northern Ireland – seemingly because of the magnificent performance of the team ... The players were tremendously brave, courageous and brilliant ...[9]

Apparently the Swedish newspaper *Idrotts-Bladet* agreed with her ladyship, naming no fewer than three Northern Ireland players in its World XI, based on performances in the tournament. The three superstars (what would they be worth now, I wonder?) were Harry Gregg in goal, Danny Blanchflower at right-half and Peter McParland at outside-left. In fact the only country to have a higher representation in this World XI was Brazil with five players (yes, Pelé was one of them). It was an accolade that required no further comment.

Northern Ireland had one last party, at the post-match banquet in Norrköping. It was attended by Frank Perssons, representing the Swedish FA, who spoke from the heart and, one suspects, for all Swedes when he proclaimed: 'I am so glad that I was chosen [as the Swedish liaison official for the Northern Ireland team] for I have never met a happier bunch of sportsmen and officials.'[10]

Malcolm Brodie described for the *Belfast Telegraph* the evening's closing emotional scene:

> And before all joined in singing 'Auld Lang Syne', Harry Gregg, the outstanding personality in the entire series, lifted the team's 'mascot', 13-year-old Bengt Jonasson, into the air.
> 'Three cheers for Bengt,' he called. Tears streamed down the cheeks of the blond Tylösand boy. And they were not far either from the eyes of the others in the party. They were sad that the end had come.[11]

In fact Northern Ireland's Swedish adventure was not quite over – there was a bit of excitement still to come, though of the sort everyone could have done without.

The IFA party was scheduled to fly back to the UK from Bromma International Airport in Stockholm and all went smoothly until the plane was in the air. Then a problem developed with the undercarriage – it would not retract. The pilot's only option was to bring the plane back down but he could not land with full fuel tanks. This meant the plane had to remain airborne, circling the airport, while the fuel was burnt up (some two hundred gallons). The operation took about an hour and a safe landing was executed as the emergency services stood by. Thoughts of Munich cannot have been far from people's minds. Eventually, aboard a fully operational aircraft, the team returned to a hero's welcome.

Fortunately, the one member of the Northern Ireland squad who had experienced the trauma of Munich was not on the aborted flight. Rather than fly to London with his team-mates and then face a second flight to Northern Ireland, Harry Gregg, at the last moment, asked Peter Doherty if he could possibly take a direct flight from Stockholm to Belfast. Doherty passed the request on to Billy Drennan and, as ever, the IFA Secretary was up to the challenge, securing seats for Gregg and IFA selector Sammy Walker, who was to accompany him, on a flight to Nutt's Corner. Gregg's flight took off before the plane carrying the rest of the team and IFA officials, so he was spared that tension and anxiety.

However, on the flight to Belfast, Gregg had his own burden to bear and it had nothing to do with this being his first time on an aircraft since the Munich crash in February. Sitting next to the Northern Ireland 'keeper on the flight was the wife of a bookie from Southampton, a woman who obviously was not allowed to speak at home. Almost from the moment they sat down, to the safe touch-down at Nutt's Corner, Gregg faced a barrage of chatter that made the attacks he had repelled in the West Germany game look like child's play. Some years later when he again met up with Walker, this episode, a most unusual finis to Northern Ireland's epic story at Sweden '58, was one of their first subjects of conversation:

> ... not long before Sammy passed away, we got talking about old times. He asked me if I remembered the woman from Southampton who bent my ear during that homeward journey from Sweden. I said: 'I think I do. I thought she was never going to shut up.'[12]

Back on home soil, Northern Ireland could bask, if only for a moment, in the glory of what they had achieved in Sweden; while Harry Gregg could at last relax in the knowledge that he had survived an opponent more formidable than Uwe Seeler.

1. Billy Bingham, *Soccer With the Stars,* The Soccer Book Club, 1964, p. 123.
2. John Camkin, *World Cup 1958,* The Sportsman's Book Club edition, 1959, p. 130.
3. *Belfast Telegraph,* 19 June 1958.
4. Ibid.
5. Ibid.
6. *Belfast News-Letter,* 23 June 1958.
7. *Belfast Telegraph,* 20 June 1958.
8. Ibid., 21 June 1958.
9. Ibid.
10. Ibid., 20 June 1958.
11. Ibid.
12. Harry Gregg, with Roger Anderson, *Harry's Game: The Autobiography,* Mainstream, 2002, p. 91.

EPILOGUE

Pelé's wonder goal against Sweden was the decisive moment of the game. From that point on, Brazil turned the World Cup final into a football carnival. They eventually ran out 5-2 winners, Pelé scoring a second, his team's final goal. The team whose name has become synonymous with World Cup success had won the trophy for the first time, a moment for all to savour, especially the precocious youth who had made that match his own:

> As the final whistle blew, ending the game and the tournament, I had a strange feeling that I was going to faint. It was over. It was finally over! And we had won! We were the champions of the world! We were the champions of the world![1]

Northern Ireland had their heroes, too, chief of whom was Harry Gregg who was named as the goalkeeper of the tournament by the watching sportswriters. It had also been a great World Cup for Peter McParland, scorer of five goals, the third-equal highest scorer in the competition with Vavá of Brazil, and still the second highest British scorer in World Cup finals competitions after Gary Lineker of England; for Billy Bingham whose thrusting runs down the right were often the launch pad for openings on the opposition goal; for Bertie Peacock who ran and tackled with seemingly endless energy; for Alfie McMichael who kept in check some of the world's best wingers; and for the versatile Wilbur Cush who attacked or defended to equal effect. Gregg hardly exaggerates when he asserts that the World Cup 'lifted Irish football to another level'.

But the real story of Sweden '58 for Northern Ireland was not about individual excellence – though that clearly existed

– but about team spirit, about a collective triumph in which players, management, reporters and supporters had combined as brothers in arms to conquer mighty foes. Terence Elliott, of the *Daily Express*, was an observer of this phenomenon, writing of:

> ... the wonderful friendship forged between these players, their manager, their officials and their accompanying journalists. And I tell other countries' representatives that here was the first lesson of sportsmanship, the first lesson of success. I have seen nothing like it in my long travels that have taken me thousands of miles to all parts of the world.[2]

Peter McParland's analysis of the team's success strikes a balance between individual ability and team cohesion:

> We always had a large number of players, good players, playing to the top of their ability in the games. We all struck up on the day. Because [most of] these lads all played in the First Division [today's Premier League]. It was the World Cup and they were inspired and they inspired themselves ... We had a lot of players playing at the top of their game during those matches in the World Cup. [All we lacked was] a goalscoring centre-forward.

Jimmy McIlroy makes the point that Northern Ireland benefited from being unburdened by the weight of expectation that other teams carried into the World Cup, many observers considering them to be simply 'making up the numbers'. That, however, in no way diminishes their achievement:

> Of course, when I look back to that Irish team now – and I say this to so many people – we were fortunate that we had so many top-class players in British football ...

most of them played at the highest level in Scotland or England ... so many of them were stars in their own particular club[s] ... I call myself lucky that I played in that era ... For some time after the World Cup, Northern Ireland was a team that went out against the home countries – England, Scotland and Wales – not feeling one bit inferior. I think that that tournament convinced us that we were the equal of any team in Britain.

When the curtain came down on Sweden '58, the world was left with indelible memories of Garrincha, Vavá, Didi and above all the seventeen-year-old Pelé. But neither would it forget the smallest of the nations to compete and their exciting encounters with the then champions of South America and champions of the world. Northern Ireland players had their day in the sun, and deservedly so: Gregg and Peacock, Blanchflower and Bingham, McIlroy and McParland.

Inevitably, comparisons are always made between the side that shone in Sweden in 1958 and their successors who reached the World Cup finals in Spain in 1982 and Mexico in 1986 (as well as winning two British Championships). Perhaps no one is better placed to make an authoritative judgement on the two teams than the man who played on the right wing in Sweden and was team manager in the glory days of the 1980s: Billy Bingham. He ponders the question about how the two sides match up for a few moments before answering:

I would think the team that I managed, overall, was more powerful. I think that would be a word I would use for them. The team that I managed had that extra power. We, in the '58 World Cup, were a mixture of people who had played [together over a period] which was a great advantage – McIlroy, myself, [Danny] Blanchflower, Peacock. We had very good ball players then. And the comparison [with the early 1980s team] is that we equally had good ball players, but we had a lot of power. When you think of those players, like Gerry Armstrong – strong. I made him into a right-winger because I wasn't getting enough from the right side and I thought Gerry would do better there, and he did. Billy Hamilton would have run through a brick wall, and Norman [Whiteside] was nineteen going on thirty. I would say [the two teams] were probably equally good – that would be the best way to sum it up. When you look at what I had in terms of Chris Nicholl, John McClelland – fast as hell; Chris Nicholl was as hard as nails; [Mal] Donaghy ... so quick on the overlaps. We had a nice combination there of speed, power and skill.

Bingham inevitably has more to say about the team of the 1980s – the era is that bit closer, the memories more vivid. Yet what he does not say about the team he managed is equally instructive in comparing those sides of the late '50s and early '80s. Although he asserts that the team he led to two World Cup final tournaments and two British Championships had 'equally good ball players' as Peter Doherty's side, he does not name them. In the case of the 1958 team, the names roll easily off the tongue – Blanchflower, McIlroy, Peacock ... And in the case of the 1980s side, he has no difficulty in illustrating its power: Armstrong, Chris Nicholl, McClelland, Donaghy ...

What Bingham's assessment suggests is that the 1958 World Cup quarter-finalists had skill, the 1982 World Cup side had strength, which is not to say that these teams lacked other qualities. In *Six Glorious Years: Following Northern Ireland 1980– 86*, I concluded that the team of the 1980s probably had the edge on the one twenty-five years earlier. I must now confess that this judgement was based on an insufficient knowledge and appreciation of the team Peter Doherty guided to the last eight of the World Cup. I would now revise my opinion to recognise that Northern Ireland has produced two great teams in its history, separated by a quarter of a century and by the style of play that they practised. And I would agree with Bingham's bottom line – that they were equally good, and the memories they have left, equally golden.

One final thought. As noted, if Northern Ireland had beaten France in the quarter-finals, their semi-final opponents would have been Brazil. Now I wonder what Pelé would have made of Wilbur Cush.

1. Pelé, *My Life and the Beautiful Game*, New English Library, London, 1977, p. 52.
2. N Ireland v. England, Windsor Park, Belfast, 4 October 1958, official match programme.

SOURCES

Interviews
Billy Bingham, 21/4/08
Harry Gregg, 28/9/07
Jimmy McIlroy, 27/3/08
Peter McParland, 19/3/08
Norman Uprichard, 27/4/08

Match Programmes
N Ireland   v British Army, 13/9/50
                v England, 7/10/50
                v Wales, 7/3/51
                v France, 12/5/51 (Festival of Britain)
                v British Army, 10/9/52
                v Scotland, 8/10/55
                v Portugal, 1/5/57
                v England, 4/10/58

UK v Europe, 13/8/55 (IFA 75th Anniversary)

Newspapers
Belfast News-Letter
Belfast Telegraph
Irish News
Northern Whig

Periodicals
New Ulster

Books
Bingham, Billy, *Soccer With the Stars*, The Soccer Book Club, 1964
Blanchflower, Danny, *The Double and Before ...*, Nicholas Kaye Limited, 1961
Bowler, Dave, *Danny Blanchflower: A Biography of a Visionary*, Victor Gollancz, 1997

Brodie, Malcolm, *100 Years of Irish Football*, Blackstaff Press, 1980

Brodie, Malcolm, *The Story of Glentoran: Official History of the Club*, Glentoran Football Club, 1981

Camkin, John, *World Cup 1958*, The Sportsman's Book Club edition, 1959

Doherty, Peter, *Spotlight on Football*, Art and Educational Publishers, 1947

Dougan, Derek, *Attack: The Autobiography of Derek Dougan*, Pelham Books, 1969

Gregg, Harry with Anderson, Roger, *Harry's Game: The Autobiography*, Mainstream Publishing, 2002

Hugman, Barry, ed., *Football League Players Records 1946–92*, Tony Williams Publications, 1992

McIlroy, Jimmy, *Right Inside Soccer*, The Sportsman's Book Club, 1961

McParland, Peter, *Going for Goal*, Souvenir Press Ltd, 1960

Nawrat, Chris and Hutchings, Steve, *The Sunday Times Illustrated History of Football*, Hamlyn, 1994

Pelé, *My Life and the Beautiful Game*, New English Library, 1977

Priestly, JB, *The Good Companions*, Penguin Books edn, 1980

Radnedge, Keir, ed., *The Ultimate Encyclopaedia of Soccer. The Definitive Illustrated Guide to World Soccer*, Carlton/Hodder and Stoughton, 1994

Robinson, Michael, *Football League Tables 1888–2003*, Soccer Books, 2003

Schindler, Colin, *Fathers, Sons and Football*, Headline, 2001

Smailes, Gordon, *The Breedon Book of Football League Records*, Breedon Books, 1991

Venables, Terry, *Terry Venables' Football Heroes*, Virgin Books, 2001

Williams, Neville, Walker, Philip and Rowett, John, *Chronology of the 20th Century*, Helicon, 1996

INDEX

Derby County 15
Distillery 9, 13, 45, 49, 50
Doherty, Peter 1, 3, 9, 11–23, 25–35, 38, 39, 41, 42, 48, 50, 52,
    55, 57, 58–61, 66, 68, 70, 71, 75, 77–80, 84, 91, 97–101,
    103, 105, 117, 118, 121, 122, 124, 126–131, 133, 135–140,
    142, 143, 145, 147, 150–153, 156, 159, 161, 163, 165,
    169–171, 173, 174, 176–179, 182, 185, 188–190, 192, 193,
    195, 197, 202, 203, 205
Dolejsi, Bretislav 133, 135, 137, 173, 175, 177
Doncaster Rovers 11, 15, 36, 49, 60, 66, 68, 71, 79, 81, 97,
    117, 121
Dougan, Derek 2, 5, 50, 96, 120, 122, 129, 130, 132, 133, 136,
    137, 142, 150, 156, 171, 205
Drennan, Billy 69, 82, 83, 85, 91, 109, 116, 123, 194, 197
Dundalk 51
Dvorak, Milan 133, 135, 138, 171, 173, 176

Edwards, Duncan 39, 79
Ellis, Arthur 83, 133, 139
England 9, 10, 13, 14, 20, 22, 25, 31, 32, 34, 36, 38, 42, 45,
    51, 52, 53, 54, 77, 78, 79, 80, 99, 117, 119, 121, 125, 128,
    139, 152, 155, 168, 172, 182, 199, 201, 203, 204
Everton 45

Ferrario, Rino 81, 87, 90, 101, 102
FIFA 81, 92, 94, 95, 108, 109, 110, 113, 114, 118, 120, 121,
    150, 170, 186
FIGC (Italian Football Federation) 79, 82, 83, 84, 94, 95, 96,
    105
Finney, Tom 31, 40
Firmani, Eddie 66, 67, 68
Foni, Dr Alphonse 79, 98
Fontaine, Juste 188, 189, 190, 192
France 30, 44, 66, 76, 119, 120, 164, 168, 173, 184–186, 188,
    189, 191–194, 203, 204

Gardbazalbal, Juan 189
Ghiggia, Alcide 80, 81, 88, 98, 101, 103–105
Glenavon 35, 40, 49, 60, 65, 66, 71, 79, 121, 192